This Old Canoe

How to Restore Your Wood-Canvas Canoe

This Old Canoe

How to Restore Your Wood-Canvas Canoe

by Mike Elliott

Photographs by Mike Elliott, James Elliott, Brittany Merry
Illustrations by Mike Elliott

KETTLE RIVER
CANOES

Cover and Book Design: Mike Elliott
Printed by CreateSpace

Published by Kettle River Canoes
7480 4th Street, P.O. Box 2324
Grand Forks, BC, V0H 1H0 Canada

ISBN 978-0-9948633-0-0

Front and back covers, title page photography: Mike Elliott.

Library and Archives Canada Cataloguing in Publication Data

Elliott, Mike, 1954-, author
    This old canoe : how to restore your wood-canvas canoe / by Mike Elliott.

ISBN 978-0-9948633-0-0 (paperback)

    1. Canoes and canoeing. I. Title.

VM353.E45 2015   623.82ʾ9   C2015-905657-8

Disclaimer:

Although certain products are recommended in this book, the author wishes to make it clear that no
one connected with the production of this book has any interest whatsoever in promoting any of the
companies mentioned. The opinions offered are based simply on what we believe to be true.

Whereas steam by its very nature is extremely hot; the inhalation of noxious fumes emitted by
volatile organic compounds contained in stains, shellacs, paints and varnishes are debilitating
to most human nervous systems; sawdust is known to cause irreversible damage to respiratory
organs; and power tools tend to feature quickly spinning and/or reciprocating cutting implements,
great caution must be exercised and safety equipment utilized when performing any of the
procedures described and/or illustrated on these pages.

This book is as precise and accurate as experience, care and responsible research could make it.
However, neither the author nor the publisher will assume any responsibility for any accident, injury
or loss that may result from errors or from following the procedures outlined in these pages.

For my brother, William.

Contents

Preface

When I was a kid, my father worked for the Canadian government as a forest entomologist (He would always refer to himself as "a real bugger"). Our whole family spent a few summers at forest research stations in north-western Ontario. That is where my father infused us with a love of canoes and canoeing. Over the course of those summers, he and I would hop into a wood-canvas canoe. He took me out on the lake and taught me how to paddle. He had grown up in Peterborough, Ontario and raced cedar strip canoes in the 1930's. My memories of those summers in northern Ontario include waking up to the sound of warblers singing in the black spruce trees, swimming in the freezing water of those lakes until my lips turned blue and watching the sunset over the lake from my position in the middle of a canvas-covered canoe.

About 36 years later, I had my head positioned inside an old 14' "Huron" canoe – my first restoration project – as I cleaned and scraped the old wood. It was given to me by Richard Reid, a professional artist living in the southern interior of British Columbia. I happened to look up and had a view of the canoe from the centre looking towards the bow. Memories came flooding back to me. This was what I saw when I was six years old – the same ribs, the same seats, the same canoe. I checked with my father. He was a skilled carpenter and knew those old canoes inside-out. Sure enough, the canoes we used at the research stations were 14' "Huron" canoes.

In my late teens, I became involved in elite-level sport and immersed myself in that – for me at least – neurotic, self-absorbed world. For the next twenty years I competed as both an athlete and a coach on national and international stages. In this environment, I gave little thought to life outside of the gymnasium. Then, I met Christy Luke in 1993 and soon decided to build a new life with her in Grand Forks, British Columbia. Yes, I had to look it up too. It was there that I decided to "get a life" and return to some of the things that brought me joy when I was a kid.

The next summer, as we looked out at the spectacular view from Chateau Lake Louise near Banff, Alberta, I turned to Christy and announced, "I am going to build a canoe and paddle it on this lake." A few weeks later,

Christy bought me a copy of Ted Moore's *Canoecraft: An Illustrated Guide to Fine Woodstrip Construction.*

At this point, I should mention that I have dyslexia. It can take me up to an hour to read a page in a book. I find the prospect of reading anything to be daunting, unless I am reading something that interests me. I also require some previous background in the topic. Without a context, the words on the page are incomprehensible to me. Fortunately, as I started into *Canoecraft,* I found that Ted Moores included lots of pictures as well as some background information about the original cedar strip canoes. This harkened back to the stories my father told me about racing those canoes in Peterborough.

I poured over the book and soon approached my co-worker Barry Pratt with an idea. We were working with a group of boys who were having a rough time making sense of themselves and their place in the world. One thing I learned during my life in sport was that our worst personal demons can be conquered when there is a something worthwhile at the end of the road.

Barry and I asked the boys if they would like to go on a canoe trip. They were thrilled, but their enthusiasm waned when we told them they were going to build the canoes first. They were sure that the project would never happen and, if it did, the canoes would be ugly and sink to the bottom of the lake. They asked us if we had ever built canoes before. We held up our copy of *Canoecraft* and said, "No, but we have a book." The boys were convinced that the project was doomed.

Five months later, as the boys paddled the finished canoes toward a campsite on Christina Lake in British Columbia, a big power boat cruised up. The men in the boat complimented us on the beautiful canoes. The boys straightened up a little. Was that a sense of pride I saw? Was there even the glimmer of self-esteem shining through? The boys replied, "Thanks, we built them."

The boys donated the canoes to a local summer camp and became minor celebrities for a time. People around town started to refer to me as "The Canoe Guy". It was then that Richard Reid gave me his old canoe. When Christy asked me if I had ever restored a canoe before, I said, "No, but I have a book."

This time, it was a copy of *The Wood & Canvas Canoe: A Complete Guide to its History, Construction and Maintenance* by Jerry Stelmok and Rollin Thurlow. They devoted one chapter to canoe restoration. It was enough to get me started and once friends-of-friends found out that I knew how to do it, I restored half-a-dozen canoes in as many years.

When I am learning something, it helps me to write about it. Fortunately, the type of dyslexia I am dealing with does not present too many problems when I am writing. In fact, I find it easier to read something when I am the one who wrote it. It also helps if I teach others while I am learning.

I helped write coaching manuals as I studied to become a professional coach. So, as I learned to restore old canoes, I kept detailed notes with a view to writing a canoe restoration manual some day. Although Stelmok and Thurlow's book was helpful, many of the situations I encountered were not addressed. By the time I started Kettle River Canoes in 2003, I had a notebook full of information that was not available in any book. The first thing I did to market my business was to post articles about canoe restoration on my website. I gave detailed instructions on some of the key aspects of the restoration process. Barry, my former co-worker, who had many years of experience in business and advertising, was appalled by my generosity. For him, I was giving away my business. He asked me why I wasn't giving away my tools too. For me, I was learning my craft and if I could help others learn at the same time, it was an added bonus. Once a coach, always a coach.

I started writing a blog about wood-canvas canoe restoration in 2009. My niece, Kristen Luke, was launching her business as a marketing consultant specializing in social media. She needed someone to practise on, so I was it. What astonished Kristen was the fact that I did everything she told me to do. The result is here in the following pages. *This Old Canoe: How To Restore Your Wood-Canvas Canoe* contains a lot of the information I shared in the blog as well as other descriptions, illustrations and photographs not published anywhere else. When Barry asks me if I am going to share all of my canoe restoration secrets, I will say, "Yes, I have a book."

Mike Elliott
Grand Forks, British Columbia

Acknowledgments

Writing a technical guide of any kind requires input, support and guidance from many people. This book would not have happened without the unwavering support of and skilled editing by my wife, Christy Luke. I followed her suggestion to begin Kettle River Canoes in 2003. Her belief in me and what I have to offer has provided me with the strength and courage to build the business and then this book. Kristin Luke, my niece and social media marketing guru, suggested I start writing an on-line blog about wood-canvas canoes. Since I began writing in 2009, she has been a constant source of encouragement and expertise. It was a delight working with Dave Carlyle, Brittany Merry and my son, James Elliott, in the shop. They kept me grounded with their energy, attention and excellent work.

Thank you to Richard Reid for giving me my first old canoe to restore, Pete Matheson for donating a number of power tools to the cause when I started the canoe restoration business and Clive Sykes for pointing out, "You are not restoring canoes for people, you are restoring the relationship people have with their canoes." Thank you to Barry Pratt for insisting on high quality work and for taking delight in my successes along the way.

One of the great advantages of writing on-line is that I have an army of technical experts, canoe historians and enthusiastic amateur restorers providing me with a treasure chest of comments, corrections and questions. Their input shaped the direction of this book and gave it a breadth and depth I could not have achieved on my own.

To all of you who have encouraged me to make this book a reality, thank you.

Introduction

Restore Your Canvas-Covered Canoe!

From This . . .

. . . To This

There is something special about wood-canvas canoes. Indeed, if you are reading this book, you are doing so because you probably grew up in canvas-covered canoes. You paddled them at summer camps; your grandfather taught you how to fish in them; your family shared wilderness adventures made possible by your faithful, old canoe. It is part of the family. The connection is hard to put into words but is as strong as any other family relationship.

These canoes have an elegance born in nature and are shaped by the elements that surround them. They are as beautiful as they are functional. They seem to move and breathe as part of the environment – part of you. However, in the latter part of the 20ᵗʰ century, aluminum and fiberglass canoes flooded the market along with their low-cost production methods. They pushed their labour-intensive canvas-covered cousins into obscurity. But family ties are strong. When a wood-canvas canoe becomes old and battered, it is carefully tucked away in the back of a shed or in the rafters of a barn. For whatever reason, most people who own wood-canvas canoes are loathe to part with them. What strikes me is that they were designed, from the outset, to be repaired and restored to their former glory.

Unfortunately, the methods and skills required for canoe restoration are from a by-gone age. In the pages that follow, my goal is not only to help you restore your canoe, but to help preserve the skills that make it possible.

This book provides the specific knowledge and techniques required to transform your old, rotten, forgotten canoe into a treasured family heirloom that can bring delight to you and others for decades to come.

Built to be Rebuilt

Your wood-canvas canoe is held together (almost exclusively) with tacks, screws and bolts. In fact, many have no glue in them at all. Consequently, any component that rots or breaks can be repaired or replaced. Once you understand the basic principles governing the behavior of wood and canvas, you will be able to rebuild your canoe.

Many years ago, my friend Richard Reid and I crawled under the back deck of his home in Christina Lake, BC to retrieve his canoe. He had not looked at it for almost 20 years and had no plans to use it again. My wife, Christy, looked at it doubtfully once we had it out on the lawn. Moss had grown a couple of inches thick and was hanging off the gunwales. Mice had chewed away the rawhide lacing in the seats as well as the better part of a couple of ribs. "Do you know how to fix it?" she asked. I smiled at her. We both knew that my woodworking skills were limited to say the least. In this, my first canoe restoration, I followed the adage: "When there is a will, there is a way". At the time, the only power tools I owned were a variable speed drill and a random-orbital sander. As it turns out, the main advantage I had was the fact that I didn't know what I was doing. All I knew for certain was that I wanted to bring this canoe back to life.

As my experience grew from weekend hobby to full-time business, I have collected more power tools and a wide assortment of specialized jigs and forms. Even so, there is one thing that is required above all else. It ensures the success of a restoration. Without it, you are doomed before you begin. A little Zen story will illustrate my point.

Zen in the Art of Canoe Restoration

A Zen master and his student were walking together across a bridge when the student asked, "Master, what is Zen?" Before the student had a chance to react, the Zen master picked him up and threw him off the bridge into the river below.

Zen is the moment – right here, right now. Zen masters have written thousands of books in an attempt to explain the unexplainable. As the student hurtled through the air towards the water in the river, he was totally consumed in the moment. No past – no future – just now.

So, what does this have to do with wood-canvas canoes? I have found that a successful canoe restoration demands a mind and body that work together in the present moment. As soon as I rush things, I make mistakes and have to start all over again. As soon as I think of myself as the expert, I find something I've never come across before. As soon as I think the task is simple, I get bogged down in complex problems. As soon as I obsess over technical aspects and try to think my way through them, everything grinds to a halt in a mass of frustration. And the more I try to get out of my head and get back to "the moment", the worse the frustrations become.

For me, a canoe restoration is an opportunity to immerse myself in the moment – now and now and now and now. When I succeed, the hammer drives the tacks straight into the wood – almost by itself. The hot, steamed wood bends to hug the canoe in a warm embrace. The work flows and I lose track of time.

However, as soon as I try to take credit for the accomplishment or repeat the masterful actions of the past, everything goes wrong. I bend a new rib over the canoe only to find that it is upside-down and has to be thrown away. The air of the shop is filled with my not-so-quiet curses.

In those moments, I endeavor to see the cloud of frustration as a gift. Sometimes at least, I am able to catch myself and laugh at the situation and – with any luck – laugh at my approach to it. I take a deep breath and shake my head. Instead of trying to change the situation, I revel in the fact that I am feeling frustrated. I practice learning how to accept the experience for what it is. When I succeed in truly embracing it – and myself – just the way it is right now, things tend to turn around. Paradoxically, as soon as I try to hold onto my feelings of frustration, they vanish and the rest of the day tends to flow a little more smoothly.

Perfection is Impossible

When it comes right down to it, you are not working *on* your old wood-canvas canoe, you are working *with* it. You and your canoe are active partners in search of a successful conclusion. You must listen to your canoe and accept its strengths and limitations. The minute you try to force the issue, your canoe will remind you who is in charge. Let your mind wander and your canoe will shake you back to reality. Think for a moment that you know what you are doing and your canoe will show you otherwise.

There will be times when you want one thing and your canoe simply has something else in mind. You must be prepared for situations where things don't go as planned. The fact is, when things work out the first time, it will be the exception rather than the rule.

Mistakes are the engine of learning and mastery. Indeed, in order to allow your body to learn anything, you must give it permission to screw up. However, you are starting down a particularly challenging path. A friend of mine, a master carpenter with 25 years experience, ran from the room a few hours into a canoe restoration and wished me luck on my crazy adventure.

Your canoe may have been made in a factory as one of thousands in the production line. However, after four or five decades, it is unique. The lines are no longer completely fair. The wood is no longer smooth and even. Abraham Lincoln said, "Every man over forty is responsible for his face." So too, the life of your canoe is written in every crack and warp in its venerable hull.

I use a lot of photographs to illustrate the techniques I describe in this book. Bear in mind that I have the luxury of selection. If I were to illustrate the mistakes as well as the successes, this book would be a twenty volume set.

My hope is that by presenting some of my successes and alerting you to some of the pitfalls, your canoe restoration will be rewarding, enjoyable and successful.

How To Use This Book

Rebuilding an old canoe is a completely different enterprise from that of building a brand new one and requires an altogether different mindset. This book is set up in a step-wise manner to help you through the entire process. The chapters are arranged in the same order you would follow in the actual restoration. The key to success is to pull your old canoe out of the shed and get to work. This book is meant to be used in the shop as you work on your canoe. Feel free to write notes in the margins. Indeed, I have provided a few pages at the back of the book for your own notes about canoe restoration procedures.

This book presents one approach to the restoration of wood-canvas canoes. I'm sure you have other ideas that work better than those discussed here. My hope is that this book provides you with a good foundation for further refinements to the process.

Chapter 1 discusses the equipment and materials required to do your project as well as a basic understanding of the wood-canvas canoe. Chapter 2 takes you through the process of assessing your canoe and planning the restoration. The restoration begins in Chapter 3 by exploring how to take your canoe apart. Chapter 4 starts the process of rebuilding your canoe by making or repairing the inwales, outwales, stems and decks. This work often involves bending wood, so that process is described in this chapter as well. The hull is restored in Chapter 5 by making or repairing ribs and planks. Seats and thwarts are discussed in Chapter 6. Chapter 7 explains how to replace the old canvas with a new one. Then, the canvas is filled, so I discuss some options for that. The chapter ends with a discussion of some alternatives to canvas. The process of making and installing a new

keel and stem-bands is explored in Chapter 8. Paint and varnish are applied in Chapter 9 followed by the final assembly and finishing details in Chapter 10.

A canoe is not fully restored until you are able to transport it safely, store it correctly and deal with minor mishaps when they occur. All of this is presented in Chapter 11. Chapter 12 provides technical dimensions for a variety of specific canoes that are each representative of many other makes and models. The book concludes with a list of resources to help make your canoe restoration a success.

The Devil is in the Details

Wood-canvas canoes are constructed with time-honoured methods and materials. However, "the devil is in the details" and it is those details that I explore in this book. Enjoy.

This Old Canoe

How to Restore Your Wood-Canvas Canoe

1
Getting Ready

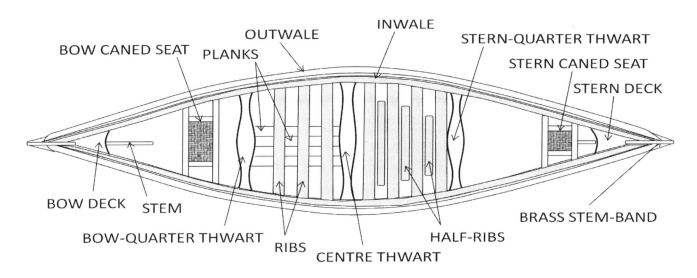

BOW CANED SEAT PLANKS OUTWALE INWALE STERN-QUARTER THWART STERN CANED SEAT STERN DECK

BOW DECK STEM BOW-QUARTER THWART RIBS CENTRE THWART HALF-RIBS BRASS STEM-BAND

(Above) Some basic canoe terminology.

Now that you have decided to restore your old canoe, there are a few things you must have in order to do the job. I will start by introducing some vocabulary. You will need to know basic canoe terminology so that you can understand the parts of your canoe and follow the directions in this book. Then, I'll discuss some of the tools, supplies and materials required for each phase of the restoration. Right now, let's look at the parts of the canoe and some basic design features.

Anatomy of Your Canoe

In general terms, a canoe is a vessel in which the paddlers are facing the same direction as they are traveling. This allows them to see what is ahead. This is critical when navigating fast-moving water flowing over and around a variey of obstacles (such as rocks, boulders and ledges). The canoe has to move just as easily backwards as forwards. Therefore, it is symmetrical – the front half is exactly the same shape as the back half.

For the canoe restorer, a symmetrical hull is extremely helpful when faced with the task of rebuilding a broken hull. As long as you have half the canoe (more or less), you can rebuild the entire thing.

It is useful to know some basic nautical terms.

Bow
The front end of the canoe is called the bow.

Stern
The back end of the canoe is called the stern.

Amidships
The centre of the canoe is referred to as both the centre and amidships.

Starboard
When in the canoe facing the bow, the right side is called the starboard side.

Port
When in the canoe facing the bow, the left side is the port side.

Other terms are used to describe the shape of the canoe. These will come into play as specific canoe designs are discussed (especially in Chapter 12). However, I will mention a few terms now that will come up a number of times in this book.

(Below) Some terminology describing the shape of a canoe hull.

Sheer-Line
The top-edge of the canoe is called the sheer-line and is delineated by the inwales and outwales (known collectively as the gunwales).

Chine
The point at which the bottom of the canoe transitions into the sides is called the chine.

Keel
The piece of wood fastened to the bottom of the canoe along the centre-line is the keel.

Rocker
The degree to which the ends of the canoe lift up beyond the bottom amidships is known as rocker.

Looking down the length of the canoe from one end to the other, the shape of the hull can change. The sides can be shaped in one of three ways.

Straight
If the sides are aligned vertically, they are called straight sides.

Flare
If the sides are angled away from the centre-line as they travel from the bottom to the sheer-line, they are said to flare.

Tumblehome
If the sides of the canoe curve back towards the centreline as they travel from the bottom to the sheer-line, they are said to have tumblehome.

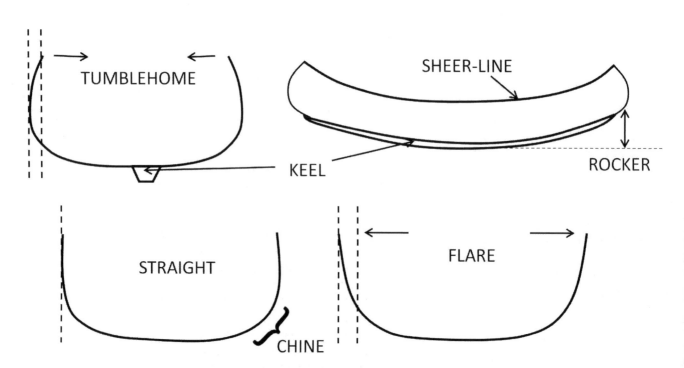

Work Space

It is not necessary to have a work shop in order to restore a canoe. All that is required is a space long enough for the canoe plus another 7' (2 meters) or so. The width of the work space need only be enough to allow you access to at least one side at a time. I restored my first canoe in my basement. The space was 8 meters long and 2 meters wide (plus a work bench).

The carport is often the workshop of choice when a dedicated space is not available. While it would be nice to have a heated space to allow work on the canoe over the winter, it is not essential. It is important to bear in mind that most of the finishes used in a canoe restoration are linseed oil-based. As a result, they need at least 10°C (50°F) to dry. The same thing applies for the glues and fillers.

For canoe restoration, floor space is more important than bench space. When I started my canoe restoration business, I didn't have a permanent work bench. Instead, I used a variety of surfaces that could fold up and be stored away when not required. I used a large, heavy folding table, a Black and Decker Workmate® and two ironing boards (all purchased at garage sales for $5 each). The ironing boards are old heavy-duty steel monsters that date back to the 1960's. They are used to support long length boards being fed onto the table saw. They also serve as portable tables when-

ever I am using a number of tools and fasteners. I set up an ironing board and a supply of fasteners on each side of the canoe. The height of the ironing board can be adjusted to allow easy access to tools that are being constantly picked up and set down again. Having the tools within inches of the work makes everything quicker and less tiring.

More recently, I have acquired a steel audio visual cart for the shop. Not so long ago, institutions and schools moved television sets and VCRs from room to room on sturdy steel carts. The TV sets were massive, heavy brutes, so the carts were built to last. In the canoe shop, they make wonderful rolling tool carts. They have large, heavy-duty wheels and are also equipped with a built-in power bar and long extension cord. These carts are no longer required in schools and often collect dust in the back corner of a storage warehouse. If you can get your hands on one, these carts are very useful in the canoe restoration shop (and elsewhere). They take up a bit of room on the floor, but you will find that you use it almost every day.

(Above) An old steel ironing board makes a handy portable table for tools around the canoe shop.

(Left) A steel audio visual cart holds all of the tools required for a specific task in the canoe restoration and rolls easily to keep everything within reach.

Safety Equipment

You will need some basic safety equipment to protect your body from head to toe:

1. respirator mask
2. safety glasses or goggles
3. hearing protection
4. work gloves
5. neoprene gloves
6. vinyl gloves

Besides the items shown, you will require a pair of coveralls or a workshop apron. My fingerless work gloves have padded leather on the palms for vibration protection. Neoprene gloves protect when working with chemical strippers and boiling water or steam. Vinyl gloves protect when applying finishes.

In addition to the personal protective equipment, be sure to outfit your shop or work space with a first aid kit, fire extinguisher (ABC type), smoke alarm and proper ventilation/dust collection.

(Right) Hearing protection and a dust mask are essential when using a random-orbital sander.

Canoe Cradles

I can still hear my dad telling us as kids, "The bottom of this canoe touches two things: air and water." Once restored, it is important to keep your old canoe off the ground between uses. You will also need some way of supporting it while you work on it. One of the most convenient systems is a pair of canoe cradles.

They are quick and simple to build and can be stored easily when not in use. They are also essential tools when repairing or refurbishing your canoe. Each one consists of two vertical struts, two base struts, two horizontal brace struts, two sling clamps and a cradle sling.

The dimensions of the cradle can vary, but all you need to build a pair of cradles are:

- 4 – 8' 2x4's (spruce)
- 2½" deck screws
- 2 strips of material 3½" wide for the slings (I use pieces of carpet or scraps of canoe canvas.)

As far as dimensions are concerned, they depend on you and your needs. Since I am 6'3" (191 cm) tall, I use cradles that are 32" (80 cm) high. My shop apprentice is 5' 3" (160 cm) tall, so she uses cradles 24" (60 cm) high. All of the horizontal brace struts are 28" (70 cm) wide. The base struts are 24" (60 cm) long. The sling material is about 50" (127 cm) long. The clamps are scrap pieces used to hold the sling material to the vertical struts. These can be about 6" long.

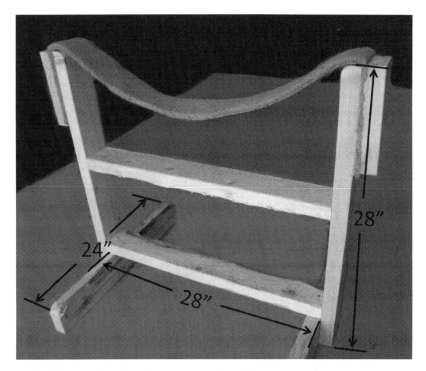

(Above) Canoe cradles are simple to build and can be done in about an hour.

To build a cradle, start by creating the sides. They each consist of a 24" (60 cm) base strut attached to one end of a 28" (70 cm) vertical strut to form a T-shape. Next, the 28" (70 cm) bottom brace strut is attached between the two sides and the 28" (70 cm) upper brace strut positioned somewhere in the middle of the vertical strut.

I take a minute to round-off the inside corners of the vertical struts. Otherwise, the sling material wears out quickly and has to be replaced frequently. I use an angle grinder and 24-grit sandpaper to round the corners, but the same job can be done with a rasp and a little elbow-grease.

Construction of the cradle is completed by attaching the sling by means of the clamps. The whole process takes the better part of an hour for both cradles. If you want to pretty them up a bit, the struts can be rounded off and sanded smooth. Any cradles that are going to spend a lot of time outside are finished with an opaque oil-based stain to protect the wood.

(Left) Component parts for canoe cradles are held together with deck screws. Start by attaching the base to the vertical strut to form a T-shape.

(Right) This wooden mallet was carved from a piece of 5/4 birch. After cutting the blank with a saber-saw, the handle was shaped with a draw knife.

A Homemade Mallet

A wooden mallet is used for a wide variety of tasks in a canoe restoration. I call mine "The Persuader" because it helps release seats from corroded carriage bolts with a little persuasion.

It is possible to buy a wooden mallet new or find one at a garage sale. However, making your own provides an opportunity to practise using tools and techniques that will be used throughout the restoration project.

I made mine from a piece of 5/4 birch (refer to page 13 for an explanation of this jargon). Actually, any dense hardwood approximately 1¼" (32 mm) thick and 3½" (89 mm) wide will make a fine mallet. Start with a piece of hardwood about 12" (30 cm) long and mark out a handle that is about half the total length. Make the width of the handle roughly the same as the thickness.

Carve the handle by first shaving the corners to create an eight-sided handle. I find that the handle is most comfortable when the body of the handle has a smaller diameter than the end. Shave each of the eight corners to create a sixteen-sided handle. Smooth the remaining

corners to create a round handle (more or less). All of this is a matter of personal preference. Once the handle feels comfortable in your hand, use some 60-grit sandpaper to smooth any ragged edges. Continue sanding in progressions from 80-grit to 220-grit to create a smooth handle. Wet the handle to raise the grain and let it dry. Hand sand in progressions from 320-grit to 600-grit. Protect the wood with a mixture of two parts double boiled linseed oil and one part turpentine. There is no need to apply varnish.

(Below) Sand off the rough edges with 60-grit sandpaper. Then, apply a mixture of two parts double boiled linseed oil and one part turpentine.

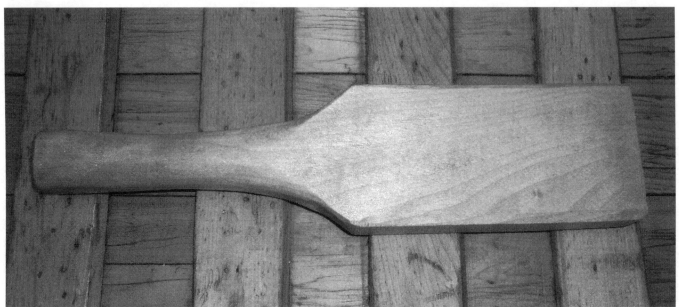

Sheer-Line Gauge

The outwales of most canoes fit flush with the top of the inwales. Consequently, the top edge of the sheer-line planks must be cut away. This is explained in more detail in Chapter 5.

They are cut to expose approximately ½" (13 mm) of the rib-tops. This can certainly be done by eye, but a simple gauge makes the job much easier. It takes a few minutes to make this gauge. Most of the dimensions are not critical.

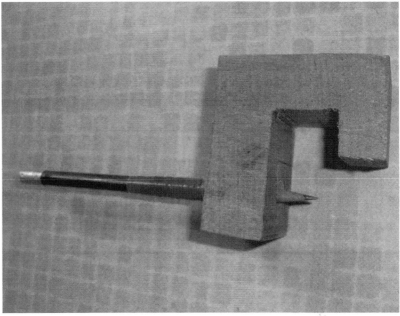

However, it is critical that the distance from the sheer-line edge of the gauge to the pencil point is ½" (13 mm). Check and recheck before you drill the hole.

I drill a 3/8" (9.5 mm) diameter hole for a standard pencil which has a ¼" (6.5 mm) diameter. I wrap some plastic electrician's tape around the pencil until I have a snug fit in the gauge.

(Above) A simple gauge is made to mark the top-edge of planking along the sheer-line.

(Left) The sheer-line gauge marks a line about 1/2" below the top of the ribs. The planks are cut along the line to expose the top 1/2" of the ribs.

(Bottom) Dimensions for a sheer-line gauge.

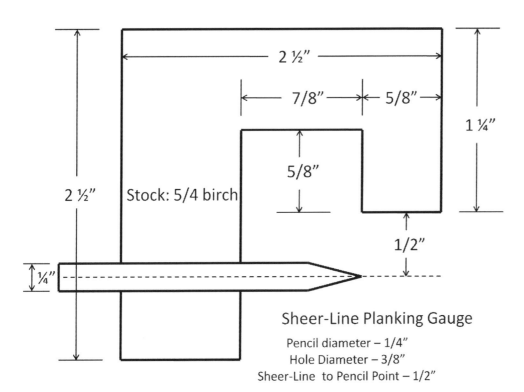

Sheer-Line Planking Gauge

Pencil diameter – 1/4"
Hole Diameter – 3/8"
Sheer-Line to Pencil Point – 1/2"

(Right) A cobbler's hammer (right) is quite different from a regular tack hammer (left).

Canoe Tack Hammer

It always helps to have the best tools for the job. Anyone restoring wooden canoes spends a lot of time hammering tacks into soft cedar. Therefore, the hammer needs to drive tacks quickly and easily without damaging the wood. I checked with the Canadian Canoe Museum as well as the Wooden Canoe Heritage Association and learned that the old-time canoe builders selected a hammer with a wide domed face. This allowed the builder to pound away on soft cedar all day without leaving any marks. Some of the old-time canoe builders forged their own hammer heads, but what they produced was essentially a cobbler's hammer. So, I went on-line and bought one on eBay for about $20.

(Below left and right) Many cobbler's hammers have a large domed face. You can pound on soft cedar without leaving a mark. This 13-ounce hammer has a face 1-3/8" (35mm) in diameter.

The face is huge – 1-3/8" (35 mm) compared to the 7/8" (22 mm) face of the previous tack hammer I bought at the hardware store. It is also heavier – 13 ounces (364 grams) compared to 10 ounces (280 grams) for the other hammer. The additional weight drives the brass canoe tacks quickly without creating fatigue after driving several hundred tacks.

The domed face creates a "sweet spot" for effective hammering. If the tack is struck near the edge of the hammer's face, the tack bends over to one side. However, with several months of practice over the course of the restoration, you will be driving tacks cleanly with only three or four hammer strokes. Soft cedar planks are left with only the slightest of impressions on the wood. You can hardly tell you've been hitting them with a hammer.

Clinching Irons

A tack hammer may be essential, but it is useless without a clinching iron. As the old song goes, "You can't have one without the other."

The traditional clinching iron for canoe restoration has a variety of curved surfaces that conform to most of the curves on the inside of your canoe. It weighs about 3.5 pounds (1.6 kg) and is 2" (51 mm) wide. The iron will cover the full width of most ribs. It can get heavy over the course of a day of tacking. However, the hole in the centre turns an otherwise unwieldy chunk of metal into a handy tool.

The traditional clinching iron does an excellent job in most situations, but it is often too large to get into the narrow confines at the ends of the canoe. While tackling my first canoe restoration, I used a small axe head and have used it ever since.

While the traditional clinching iron is beautifully designed, it is not the easiest thing to find. I restored several dozen canoes before getting a *bona fide* canoe clinching iron from Northwoods Canoe Co. in Atkinson, Maine. Until then I managed very well with a set of auto-body "dollies" available at any automotive supply shop. They often come in a set along with a variety of auto-body hammers which can serve well enough for driving canoe tacks until you acquire a cobbler's hammer.

The technique of clinching canoe tacks takes time to develop into smooth, efficient movements. The tack is pushed into the cedar plank on the outside of the canoe with your "hammering" (dominant) hand while the iron is positioned on the rib directly opposite with your "clinching" (non-dominant) hand.

(Right) A traditional canoe tack clinching iron is 2" (51 mm) wide and weighs 3.5 pounds (1.6 kg).

Check to make sure the clinching iron is in full contact with the rib and properly positioned to meet the tack. Drive the tack with authority until the head of the tack is flush with the plank. Raise the iron and run a finger over the wood at the spot where the tack came through the rib. Check to make sure the tack is not "proud" – raised above the rib. If you can feel the tack above the wood, the iron was not in full contact with the rib at the point where the tack came through. Reposition the iron and give the head of the tack another hit with the hammer. Raise the iron again and do another check.

Positioning of the iron is crucial to getting a proper "clinch" in the tack. When driving tacks on the bottom of the canoe, it helps to have an assistant holding the iron while you tack. Communicate with each other to make sure you are both working at the same location on the same rib at the same time. It takes time to develop a comfortable rhythm. Usually by the time you have your technique down, the project is completed. Nonetheless, it is a satisfying activity when things are going well. On the other hand, be prepared for lots of frustrations and keep your tack remover close by to pull out bent tacks.

(Below left) An old axe head clinches canoe tacks in the narrow confines at the ends of the canoe.

(Below right) Auto-body "dollies" make excellent canoe tack clinching irons.

(Right) Position the planking gauge with the hook-end grabbing the tapered side of the space in which the new piece of planking will fit.

Planking Gauge

As mentioned earlier, the curve of the hull where it transitions from the bottom to the side is called the chine. The planks in this area are tapered to fit the space that is roughly in the shape of a football. Replacing them requires precise measurement.

One end of the planking gauge is bent to form a right-angled hook. Place this hook to grab the tapered side of the space where the new piece of planking will fit. Place the new plank into the space with one edge sitting flush along the non-tapered side of the hole. The other edge of the plank overlaps the space and needs to be cut to fit precisely into the hole. The gauge holds the excess plank in the "U-pocket" of the tool with the notched end on top.

Run a pencil line along the edge of the notch to mark the position of the tapered edge of the plank. Move along the tapered edge of the hole to mark at regular intervals until you have travelled the full-length.

Remove the new plank and use a straight edge to join the marks into a line that describes the tapered edge of the plank. Cut along the line with a utility knife to create the desired piece. It is a good idea to cut a little outside the line and shave it off as necessary until the new piece is an exact fit. It takes less time to mark and cut the new plank than it does to explain how to use the gauge.

(Below) The planking gauge is a strip of brass bent into a U-shape with a right-angled hook on one end and a notch formed at the other end.

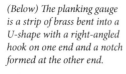

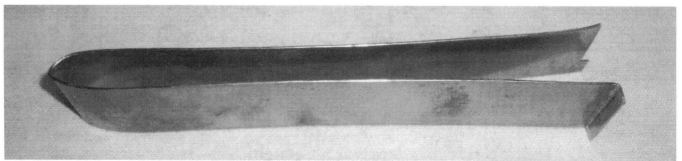

(Right) Mark the location of the tapered edge of the new planking at regular intervals along the full-length of the new plank.

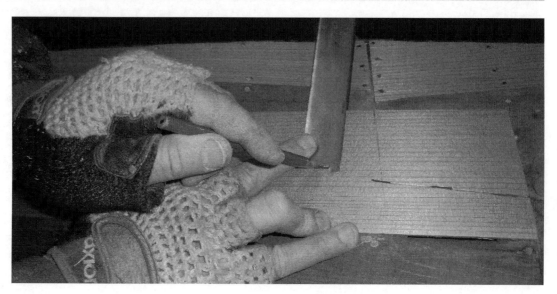

Wood

Most people prefer to end up with their canoe looking exactly like it was when it was built many decades earlier. Usually, this involves using the same woods that were used in the original construction. In some cases this is not possible. For example, all-wood cedar strip canoes built in the early 1900's have ribs made of rock elm which is now close to extinction. Other woods are hard to come by. An example of this, is cedar.

Without a doubt, eastern white cedar (*Thuja occidentalis*) is the best wood for canoe construction. It is light, strong, resists rot and bends beautifully when soaked and steamed. In addition, it does not split when brass canoe tacks are driven into it to hold planking to ribs. When it comes time for the canoe restorer to remove tacks from 40-year-old white cedar, very little damage results.

By comparison, western red cedar (*Thuja plicata*) is more prone to splitting when canoe tacks are driven into it and older planking breaks more easily when tacks are removed from it. It resists rot and bends well – although not as well as eastern white cedar.

For many wood-canvas canoes, eastern white cedar was the only wood used to construct the hulls. However, as the supply of good quality white cedar became harder to come by in the late 1960's and early 1970's, many companies turned to the abundant supplies of western red cedar for the planking of their canoes. Bill Greenwood, who built canoes in Richmond, BC from 1934 to 1975, used western red cedar exclusively for the planking in his canoes.

As a canoe restorer in British Columbia, I use western red cedar for my repair work. It is abundant, reasonably priced and I can get it custom-milled locally. The difficulty is getting wood with perfectly straight grain. It is the main reason I get my wood custom-milled. It matches very well to the older wood in the rest of the hull. I always have to stain new wood to darken it to match the original wood. In the end, it is difficult to tell which ribs are the originals and which are the replacements.

Wood is ready to become seats, decks and gunwales. "4/4" refers to a board that is 1" (25 mm) thick.

It is interesting to note that Bill Greenwood used sitka spruce (*Picea sitchensis*) for the ribs of his canoes. At the time he was building, sitka spruce was widely available on the west coast of British Columbia. Now, it is very expensive and much harder to come by, so I use western red cedar to replace broken ribs in Greenwood canoes. I suppose the purist would have a hard time with this type of substitution. Essentially, it comes down to a choice on your part.

In some cases, authenticity gives way to practical considerations. You may decide that the original wood was not the best choice for a particular component in your canoe. I have replaced original decks made of western red cedar (in Richardson canoes) with hardwood (such as oak) to create a stronger, more durable canoe. I have also replaced original oak decks with birds-eye maple because I happened to have a scrap piece left over from another project and liked the idea of making the canoe a little prettier.

When you go to the lumberyard, there is a piece of wood jargon that comes in handy when making your order (in North America). They talk about the thickness of a board in multiples of 1/4". For example, "four-quarters maple" refers to a maple board that is 1" (25 mm) thick (4 x 1/4"). This is written as 4/4 maple. Therefore, 5/4 birch refers to a board of birch that is 1-1/4" thick. The actual thickness of the board depends on whether or not the board is rough or planed, so be sure to ask about that as well.

13

(Above right) An exterior-grade wood filler can patch gouges and holes in the canoe hull.

Adhesives

Adhesives and wood fillers play a limited role in the restoration of your wood-canvas canoe. I suppose the true purist would not use them at all. However, I find they come in handy for some tasks.

In general, adhesives are used for repairing the rotted ends of inwales, outwales or stem-tops. New wood is joined to the original wood with a scarf joint. The joint is held with waterproof glue. This limits your choices.

(Below right) Waterproof glues serve a limited, but useful role in the restoration of a canoe.

When joining hardwood (such as inwales and outwales), polyurethane glues reign supreme. They hold very well, fill gaps and sand smooth. I use a polyurethane glue for most of my hardwood joints. Follow the directions on the container. It is, essentially, expand-able foam. The moistened wood activates the glue which then foams up and sets in a few hours. Let it cure overnight before sanding. Clean up is best done with a little lacquer thinner on a rag. I do not use this glue on cedar joints. To secure scarf joints in cedar (usually in rib-top repairs), I use resorcinol glues. They are water-based and yet are waterproof. They set up in about 24 hours. Resorcinol glues bond very well, clean up with a damp rag and sand beautifully once cured. I use either Dural Marine Glue (comes in powder form that you mix with water prior to use) or Elmer's Waterproof Wood Glue (comes in a pre-mixed bottle). If you ask the people at the hardware store for resorcinol glue, they just stare at you blankly. Just look for a water-based waterproof glue.

(Left) Wood damaged by old fasteners can be solidified with a wood hardener and then filled with a two-part epoxy putty.

Any holes or gouges in original planking (created in the process of rebuilding stem-ends or replacing ribs) can be filled with an exterior-grade wood filler. I use Lepage Wood Filler. It is economical, sets up in a few hours, sands easily and creates a smooth surface prior to re-canvassing.

Sometimes the original wood is left weak-ened by holes and gouges. These are repaired in a two-step process. First, the wood is painted with a wood hardener. It penetrates deep and sets up in about 24 hours at room temperature to stabilize the original wood. There are a number of products on the market and each is handled differently. Some are water-based while others are epoxy products. The second step is to fill the holes and gouges with a two-part epoxy putty. This product usually comes in the form of a cylinder with the resin at its core surrounded by an outer layer of hardener. Pinch off as much as you need, then knead the two parts together until they are mixed evenly. You have about an hour of working time before the putty begins to set and harden. The hardened putty sands easily and accepts stain. This process of wood stabilizing and filling also works well on the original stems to fill holes left by tacks used in the previous canvas job.

Fasteners

Wood-canvas canoes are held together, almost exclusively, with tacks, screws and bolts. Therefore, selecting the correct fasteners for the canoe is an essential part of a successful canoe restoration.

Canoe Tacks

It is impossible to talk about wood-canvas canoes without talking about canoe tacks.

They are made of either copper or brass and are specifically designed for holding a canoe together – narrow, four-sided and tapered to a needle-sharp point. This shape allows them to be driven into cedar without splitting the wood.

The head of a canoe tack is small and often slightly domed. When it is driven into the wood, the bulk of the head is buried below the surface.

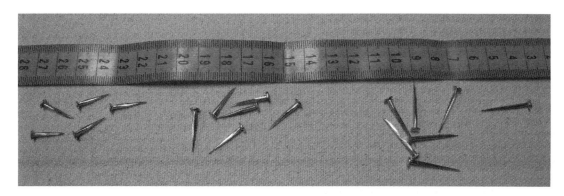

(Left) Canoe tacks come in a variety of lengths. (from left to right: 16 mm, 19 mm and 22 mm.)

Length (inches)	Length (mm)	Use of the tack in the canoe
5/8	16	To secure stretched canvas at the stems. To attach planks to the stems. To clinch 5/32" (4 mm) planks and 5/32" (4 mm) ribs together.
3/4	19	To clinch 5/32" (4mm) planks and 5/16" (8 mm) ribs together.
7/8	22	To clinch 5/32" (4 mm) planks and 3/8" (10 mm) ribs together. To attach rib-tops to inwales.

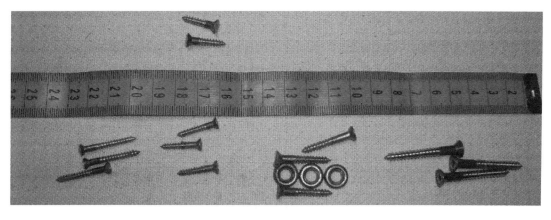

(Left) Flat-head wood screws are required in a variety of sizes and lengths. They are used to attach decks, stembands, keels and outwales.

Flat-head wood screws

These screws are used to attach a variety of components in the canoe. In the United States, slotted screws are used almost exclusively while Canadian builders tended to prefer Robertson (square-drive) screws. In the old days, the screws were made of heavy naval brass (69% copper, 1% tin and 30% zinc). The addition of tin in the alloy helped prevent the loss of zinc when exposed to saltwater for extended periods. You can reuse the original screws from the canoe or buy screws made of silicon bronze.

15

Size	Length (inches)	Length (mm)	Use of the Screw in the Canoe
#4	¾ & 1	19 & 25	Secures stem-bands (3/8" wide) to the stems.
#6	¾ & 1	19 & 25	Secures stem-bands (1/2" wide) to the stems.
#6	1	25	Secures the keel to the centre-line of the canoe (with #6 finish washers).
#8	1½	37	Secures the outwales to the sheer-line of the canoe.
#8	1¾	44	Secures the decks to the ends of the canoe.

(Below) Silicon bronze carriage bolts (#10-24) are used to attach seats and thwarts to the inwales.

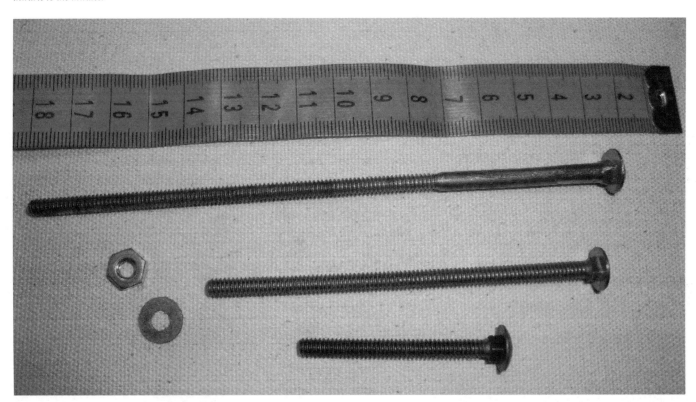

Carriage bolts

These bolts are used to attach thwarts and seats to the inwales of the canoe. Most of the original bolts I have come across were made of galvanized steel. These tend to corrode over time, so I opt for carriage bolts made of silicon bronze. The size of the bolts is unique to canoes. Therefore, 3/16" or #10-24 (4.8 mm) silicon bronze carriage bolts are commonly referred to as "canoe bolts". It should be noted that the Old Town Canoe Company uses its own style of bolt. It is a 7/32" or #12-24 (5.5 mm) brass carriage bolt with a diamond-shaped head.

Length (inches)	Length (cm)	Use of the Carriage Bolt in the Canoe
2	5	Secures the thwarts to the inwales.
4	10	Secures the seats to the inwales (with wood spacers) to hang about ¾" (22 mm) or 1¾" (44 mm) below the inwales.
6	15	Secures the seats to the inwales (with wood spacers) to hang about 2¾" (70 mm) or 3¾" (95 mm) below the inwales.

Nails

Non-corrosive fasteners (brass, bronze, copper) are essential in wood-canvas canoes. Years of exposure to water tend to corrode ferrous (steel) fasteners and result in the canoe falling apart. Alternatively, corroded ferrous fasteners become fixed in place over time. It is very difficult to remove these fasteners, so please be kind to the next person who restores your canoe and use non-ferrous fasteners.

You may notice that there are a number of options for attaching the rib-tops to the inwales. Copper common nails are the most authentic but are very soft and tend to bend even after pre-drilling. Bronze annular ring nails are very good but have to be pre-drilled. My own preference in original inwales is a 7/8" (22 mm) canoe tack. They drive easily and do not require pre-drilling. When driving nails into new ash inwales, I often have to pre-drill and use bronze annular ring nails.

Gauge	Length (inches)	Length (mm)	Metal	Use of the Nail in the Canoe
16	7/8	22	brass	These finish nails secure the gunwale-caps to the inwales in "Huron" canoes.
14	7/8	22	bronze	These annular ring nails secure the rib-tops to the inwales (pre-drilled).
14	7/8	22	copper	These common nails secure the rib-tops to the inwales (pre-drilled).

(Below) Non-corrosive nails (from left to right: silicon bronze, brass and copper) are used to attach rib-tops to inwales.

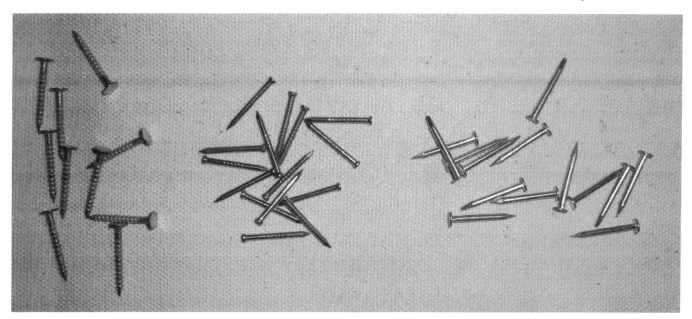

(Left) Brass finish nails attach the gunwale-cap to the inwale in "Huron" canoes. They are a marked improvement over the original steel nails that corroded quickly.

17

(Right) Apply a mixture of two parts double boiled linseed oil and one part turpentine to revitalize old wood and to help prevent water from absorbing into all of the wood.

Finishes

Bare wood has to be protected against water and rot with some kind of finish. Let's look at them in turn.

Linseed oil - Revitalize

This oil is usually sold as 'double-boiled' linseed oil. It is not actually boiled. Drying agents are added to shorten the drying time to a matter of weeks (as opposed to raw linseed oil which takes decades to dry).

To revitalize wood, mix two parts oil with one part turpentine. This allows it to spread better and penetrate the wood. Some people heat the mixture prior to application. I don't see a lot of difference as long as you are working at room temperature. Apply it liberally – there are no points for neatness. Then stand back and admire your handiwork. Personally, I usually just stand there with my mouth open – perhaps even giggling a little. Once you're done, store the canoe for at least two weeks to dry at room temperature. The temperature has to be at least 10°C (50°F).

Stain - Match original colour

In a restoration, it helps to match the colour of the new wood with that of the original. When I'm staining woods with open grain (such as oak and ash), I stain the grain with a dark brown after applying a light brown. This replicates the weathered look in the original wood. Apply the stain and wipe off any excess. Any stain is fine although I prefer gel stains when I can get them.

(Left) Pre-mixed shellac is diluted 1:1 with lacquer thinner to create a 2-pound cut that does not become cloudy when exposed to water.

Shellac - Base for varnish

Shellac is basic to all finishing. It is a resin secreted by the female lac bug on trees in the forests of India and Thailand. It is processed and sold as dry flakes which are dissolved in denatured alcohol to make liquid shellac.

Many people will caution against using shellac as a base for varnish or they will tell you that shellac goes cloudy when it comes in contact with water - not a good thing for a canoe. I researched the methods used by old canoe builders and found that most of them used shellac as a base for varnish. They had a trick for stopping it from turning cloudy that I will share in Chapter 9. Shellac is easy to use and buffs quickly with steel wool. Also, it dries in about an hour at room temperature as opposed to a couple of days for varnish. I apply two coats of shellac and a coat of varnish to new wood in one day.

Canvas Filler - Base for paint

In Chapter 7, I will describe two methods for "filling" the canvas. This process uses a compound to "size" or waterproof the canvas. When dry, the filler creates a base for the application of the oil-based paint. Without it, the paint soaks into the canvas and makes an ugly mess.

One filler is an oil-based concoction shared by the Wooden Canoe Heritage Association. I used it for years with great results. The original builders used "secret" formulations usually involving white lead. The oil-based filler from the WCHA uses silica rather than white lead. This makes it less toxic but still requires a degree of caution.

The other filler is a waterborne latex compound that is specifically designed to waterproof canvas. It contains fungicides to help prevent rot and is used in commercial and industrial buildings to "lag" or seal canvas wrappings around large airduct systems. The main advantage of this compound is the fact that it takes about 30 hours to dry instead of about 30 days for the oil-based filler.

Spar Varnish - Wood finish
Traditionally, spar varnish was made by cooking an oil (usually tung oil, linseed oil, cotton seed oil or soybean oil) with one or more resins or gums (such as shellac flakes, mastic, rosin, amber, copal or damar). These days, commercially manufactured spar varnish adds alkyd resins (derived from petrochemicals) to linseed oil. If used straight from the can, the high proportion of solids (resin) in the varnish result in a finish full of brush-marks, bubbles and sags because it takes a long time to cure.

In order to get an even finish, the curing time must be reduced. This is done by thinning the varnish about 12% with mineral spirits – a.k.a. paint thinner. In some high quality

spar varnishes, more thinner is required to get the desired curing time. Some manufacturers confuse the issue by selling products under a variety of names such as "Oil Finish", "Wiping Varnish" or "Danish Oil". In some cases, they are little more than thinned varnish.

(Above) The secret to getting a smooth, even finish in spar varnish is to thin it 12% with paint thinner.

Alkyd Enamel - Canvas finish
The filled canvas is painted with oil-based alkyd enamel paint. From a practical standpoint, you can think of alkyd enamel as pigmented varnish. Paint manufacturers would cringe at this description, but both enamel and varnish are handled in almost the same way.

These oil-based paints (often marketed as "rust paint") replaced lead-based products. They are made with synthetic alkyd resins derived from petro-chemicals. They are strong, flexible and durable. Recent changes in the regulation of volatile organic compounds (VOC's) in Canada have made oil-based paints a little more difficult to obtain. Most oil-based 'rust' paints in Canada now have a label stating "For Metal Use Only". I heard one canoe restorer remark that it must have been a clerical error that left "Canoe Use" off the label.

(Left) Oil-based alkyd enamel (often called "rust paint") creates a strong, durable and flexible finish for the canvas. As with spar varnish, it applies easily when thinned 12% with paint thinner.

(Right) A marine bedding compound seals keels and stem-bands.

Bedding Compound - Seal for decades

You will spend a lot of time and effort to create a waterproof canvas cover for your canoe. Therefore, it seems a little strange to poke a dozen or more holes through the bottom of the canoe in order to install a keel. If you do, it is essential to use a bedding compound that creates a waterproof seal and stays flexible for decades.

Having tried a variety of products, I have returned to the old school. Dolphinite 2005N Natural Bedding Compound is a linseed oil-based compound with the consistency of peanut butter. It is the same as the bedding compounds used a century ago. Other more modern compounds (such as 3M 5200 or Interlux 214) dry more quickly leading to cracks in the seal which allow water to seep into the canoe.

Wax - Protect

Don't tell anyone, but one of my trade secrets is to apply a coat of carnauba (pronounced car-NOO-bah) wax to the newly painted canvas. It is a very hard wax that protects the finish. It also helps the canoe shoot through the water effortlessly. I guarantee you will be amazed with the difference it makes.

(Left) Carnauba wax protects the newly painted canvas.

I use carnauba wax in a paste form. It is available at most automotive supply stores. Follow the directions for application and be sure to use lots of clean cloths. Using flannel and fleece rags, I move quickly over the entire canoe and keep turning the rags to a clean surface until I achieve a beautifully buffed finish.

(Bottom) The painted canvas on this Peterborough Champlain 'High-Ender' circa 1955 is protected with a coat of carnauba wax.

20

It was fine until a tree fell on it

A few months after starting my canoe restoration business, a man brought his canoe to the shop. He was not interested in having it restored but thought I could find someone who would like a nice little canoe. As he took the canoe off the roof rack of his car, he said, "It was fine until a tree fell on it."

A client came to the shop a few months later and paid for the restoration of this lovely 14' "Huron" canoe. This project confirmed for me the fact that very few wood-canvas canoes are beyond hope.

2
Assess and Plan

In order to reach a goal, the best place to start is to figure out where you are now. Therefore, in a canoe restoration, that means determining the condition of the canoe. From there, you will be able to plan the overall project. It is a good idea to write it all down. I've provided a work chart at the end of the chapter to help keep things organized and make it official. This chapter begins by giving you a context for what you may encounter as you examine your canoe. So, let's look at how your canoe was built in the factory decades ago.

How Your Canoe Was Built

Understanding how your canoe was built in the factory is essential in order to plan the restoration project. Once you know how the components were assembled and the sequence of construction, you can anticipate the kind of work required in the restoration.

Most of the canoe is made of cedar (eastern white cedar and/or western red cedar) which is strong, light-weight and rot-resistant. The hull of a 16' canoe will have approximately 45 cedar ribs oriented laterally (the length extending from one side of the canoe to the other) and stationed evenly along the length

of the canoe. The ribs are attached to cedar planks that run longitudinally (the length running from one end of the canoe to the other). This combination of lateral ribs and longitudinal planks creates the hull of the canoe. The shape of the canoe is maintained by a number of structural components – inwales, outwales, stems, decks, thwarts, seats and an optional keel. They are usually made of hardwood (ash, oak, mahogany, maple).

The canoe was constructed up-side down on a solid wood mould with steel bands positioned at each rib location. First, inwales and stems were set into place on the mould

(Right) The canoe hull is built on a solid wood mould fitted with steel bands at every rib station.

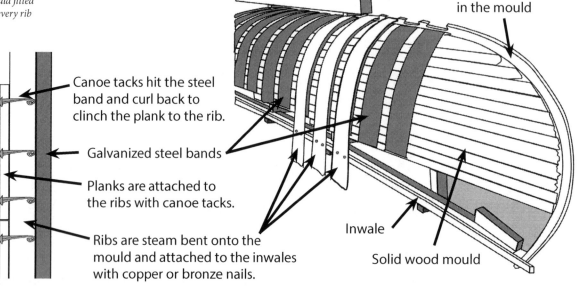

Pre-bent stem seated in the mould

Canoe tacks hit the steel band and curl back to clinch the plank to the rib.

Galvanized steel bands

Planks are attached to the ribs with canoe tacks.

Ribs are steam bent onto the mould and attached to the inwales with copper or bronze nails.

Inwale

Solid wood mould

(Above) Canoe tacks are hammered through the planks and ribs. They hit the steel bands on the mould and curl back to clinch the planks and ribs together.

(Below) Short "cant ribs" on each side of the canoe are angled or "canted" and wedged into the stem.

where the rest of the hull (cedar ribs and planks) could be attached to them. The inwales run longitudinally on either side of the canoe to form the top rail on either side. The hardwood stems were soaked for about 72 hours and then heated with steam or nearly boiling water to allow them to bend onto forms (separate from the building mould). After drying for another 72 hours, they were installed on the mould.

The cedar ribs were soaked for about 24 hours and then heated with steam or nearly boiling water for about 45 minutes. They were typically about 2" (5 cm) wide and 3/8" (9 mm) thick. Once pliable, the ribs were bent

over the mould at each rib station (on top of each steel band) with about 2" (5 cm) space between each rib. Using a tack hammer, the builders drove two 7/8" (22 mm) copper or brass nails through the top of each rib into the inwales on either side of the canoe. Each rib is about 40" to 60" (100 to 150 cm) long, depending on its position in the canoe.

There were about 16 rows of planks in the canoe. They were typically about 3" (76 mm) wide and 5/32" (4 mm) thick. To bend around the compound curves of the mould, the planks were soaked for about 10 minutes and heated with steam or nearly boiling water for about 2 minutes. The builders secured the planks to the ribs with about 2,500 brass or copper tacks ¾" (19 mm) long. The tacks were driven with a tack hammer through the plank and rib until it hit the steel band on the mould. The point of each tack was turned by the steel to clinch it into the rib and hold the two pieces together.

Once the main part of the canoe was built, it was removed from the mould. Then, the ends were assembled. The deck was attached to the inwales and, the ends of the inwales were attached to the stem. At the ends of the canoe, short ribs on each side of the hull were angled or "canted" and wedged into place. These "cant ribs" were sometimes wider and thinner than the rest of the ribs in the canoe. Sometimes, they covered one of the screws

used to attach the deck to the inwales. Therefore, when repairing rotted ends, the cant ribs must be removed first in order to access the screws that hold the deck in place.

To make the canoe waterproof, canvas was stretched over the hull and tacked in place at every rib-top with 1" (25 mm) brass or copper tacks. The end seams of the canvas envelope were closed using brass or copper tacks 5/8" (16 mm) long driven into the stem at each end. Then, the canvas was waterproofed. Each manufacturer had their own secret formula, but they included

boiled linseed oil and white lead. This "canvas filler" was applied with a brush and rubbed smooth by hand with a canvas mitt. The canoe was then set aside for at least four weeks to allow the oil to dry. Some companies had large drying rooms, hot enough to dry the filler in about half the time required at room temperature.

If the canoe was fitted with a keel longitudinally at the centre-line, it was attached with about 18 brass or bronze #6 wood-screws – 1" (25 mm) long – and finish washers. The screws were driven through the cedar ribs and planks as well as the canvas into the hardwood keel. Then the canvas seams over each stem were protected with brass stem-bands which were attached with about 8 brass or bronze #4 wood screws ¾" (19 mm) or 1" (25 mm).

(Above) Canvas is stretched over the hull in a ballet of vertical and horizontal tension. It is then tacked in place at every rib-top.

(Left) A brass strip is attached at either end to protect the canvas seam.

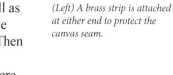

(Right) Thwarts were attached directly under the inwales with carriage bolts.

(Right) Many canoe companies attached the seats to the inwales using carriage bolts and wood spacers.

Hardwood seats (one bow seat and one stern seat) were constructed in a variety of ways. They were usually made of hardwood slats or a hardwood frame woven with either natural cane or rawhide (babiche). Woven seats took several hours to complete. Then, they were installed in the canoe by hanging them below the inwales with 4" (10 cm) 10-24 bronze or brass carriage bolts and hardwood spacers.

Hardwood thwarts were installed to help maintain the shape of the canoe. A typical 16' (5 meter) canoe was outfitted with a centre-thwart (or portage yoke) and a stern-quarter thwart. The number and arrangement of thwarts depended on the length of the canoe. They were positioned laterally and attached to the under-side of the inwales with 2" (5 cm) 10-24 brass or bronze carriage bolts running through the inwales. The outwales were positioned longitudinally on the outside of the canoe at the rib-tops to protect the top edge of the canvas. They were attached with about 50 brass or bronze #8 wood screws – 1.5" (37 mm) long.

The filled canvas was then painted with two coats of marine enamel while all of the exposed wood was usually protected with two coats of spar varnish. The enamel and varnish were both allowed to dry for 48 hours between coats.

For the restorer, it is important to bear in mind that some builders (including Huron, Richardson and late-model Chestnuts) used ferrous fasteners instead of non-corrosive brass or bronze in many of the stages of construction. These corrode and often break apart completely over the course of several decades.

It is also important to note that the canoe was assembled before the wood and canvas was protected with paint and varnish. As a result, many unprotected surfaces were susceptible to rot.

With this basis of understanding, you can examine your canoe knowing what to expect. You will be able to anticipate some of the damage and decay in your canoe as you take it apart and plan the restoration.

(Below) Most canoe companies applied two coats of marine enamel to the filled canvas.

Surveying Your Canoe

Your canoe is now sitting in your work space and you are about to start the restoration. The first step is to assess the condition of the canoe in order to then prepare a plan for the project. As an example, let's look at a Chestnut Prospector that came into the shop a few years ago.

This Prospector had seen better days, but the full extent of the damage was not apparent until it was taken apart – at least a little. I started by removing the screws holding the outwales to the rest of the canoe. Many canoes have had regular coats of varnish applied over the years, so the outwales seem perfect. However, as mentioned earlier, the inside surface of the outwales was unprotected and susceptible to rot. In about 60% of restorations, the outwales have to be replaced. Such was the case in this canoe.

Removing the outwales also exposes the canvas. If the canvas is original (i.e. at least thirty or forty years old), it also needs to be replaced. Such was the case with this 45 year old canoe.

The stem-ends are highly susceptible to rot. Water is trapped under the stem-band where the inwales, stem-end and deck come together. At the writing of this book, I have restored over 170 canoes. Of those, only a handful did not have rot in the ends. In this Prospector, it was clear that all of the components would have to be rebuilt. When contemplating your canoe restoration, bank on having to rebuild the ends and perhaps replace the decks as well.

(Above) This Chestnut Prospector has seen better days.

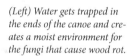

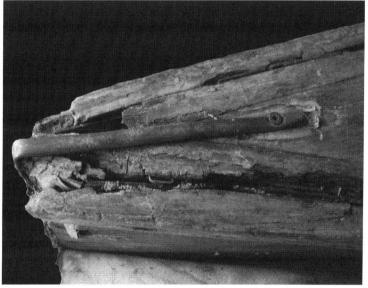

(Left) Water gets trapped in the ends of the canoe and creates a moist environment for the fungi that cause wood rot.

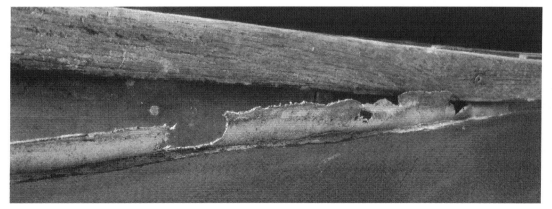

(Bottom) The bare canvas under the outwales rots and tears away.

(Above left) Expose the ends of the canoe to determine the full extent of the damage.

(Above right) Careful inspection is required to find all of the broken ribs.

To assess the damage, remove the stemband, peel back the canvas and remove the planking to expose the top of the stem. I prefer to leave most of the canvas attached to the canoe at this point. It helps contain cleaning and stripping chemicals when I start the restoration.

In most Chestnut and Peterborough wood-canvas canoes, the inwales and outwales were constructed with two pieces of ash and a scarf joint. Over the years, it usually lets go. This is not a big deal and can be easily repaired.

Many canoes come into the shop with the outwales missing entirely. You can replace them with a generic component available from most professional canoe builders. I prefer to replicate the original outwale for a specific canoe. It takes longer but maintains the original look.

When examining the hull of the canoe, be prepared to spend a few hours checking every rib and plank carefully. Sometimes broken ribs are obvious, but usually the only indication is a bulge in hull. In the case of this Prospector, I found only one broken rib. That said, it is common to discover a couple more once the old varnish is removed and all of the cracked wood is clearly visible.

(Below left) Scarf joints in the original gunwales often separate. A simple re-gluing is often all that is required.

(Below right) Many canoe seats are hand-woven with rattan or laced with rawhide. Your first attempt at re-weaving the seats may take several days.

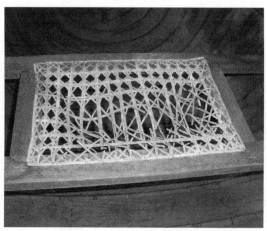

(Above left) Original slat seats are relatively easy to repair and refinish. The original carriage bolts are corroded.

The slat seats in this Prospector will be restored by stripping the old varnish and rebuilding the finish. The carriage bolts are galvanized steel and have corroded. I will replace them with silicon-bronze bolts, washers and nuts.

A quick glance at this canoe shows warped gunwales. This happens when it has been well used or if it was set down on one side for years. The only way to restore the fair lines is to replace both the inwales and the outwales. This is a huge job requiring you to take the entire canoe apart and put it back together. It is up to you to decide whether it is worth the effort.

The interior varnish is often in good shape and requires nothing more than a good cleaning and scrubbing followed by a couple of coats of spar varnish. In this canoe, the varnish is cracked, flaking and, in some places, gone all together. I'll remove the old varnish and rebuild the finish.

(Below left) Original inwales are often no longer fair. Replacing them is an enormous job.

(Right) When original varnish is cracked and flaking, it is time to strip the old varnish and rebuild the finish from the ground up.

(Right) Original stem-bands can often by reused. In this case, the originals were replaced with a make-shift metal strip.

In many canoes, I have to contend with repairs made by other people. I spend a lot of time removing fiberglass, lag-bolts, silicon and gobs of epoxy. In this case, I will remove the old repairs and restore the original look of a Chestnut Prospector.

I can often re-install the original stem-bands. However, in this canoe I will have to replace the stem-bands with exact replicas of the originals.

I will match the new paint with the original light-green colour that the Chestnut Canoe Company called "grey". They used it on their working canoes (Prospector, Ogilvy, Cruiser and Freighter). Also, many people want to replace the original decals. They are available for many of the big companies such as Chestnut, Peterborough, Old Town and Penn Yan. This Prospector will be fitted out with new decals on the deck and hull.

(Left) You may spend a lot of time dealing with repairs made by other people. In this case, the end of the deck and the ends of the inwales were cut off and replaced by one solid chunk of wood to fill the void.

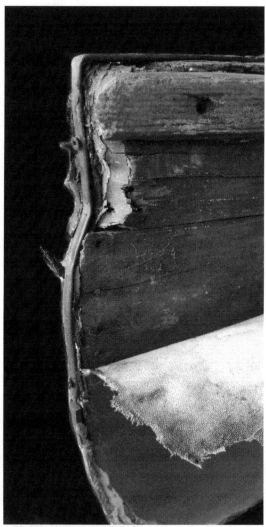

As you assess your canoe, it is useful to keep track of the work that needs to be done. You will also be formulating a plan of attack. So, let's look at the steps involved in a restoration and the sequence of events. My sequence is not a definitive one. For example, some restorers install the stem-bands after the canvas is painted while I install them and then paint. It all comes down to personal preference.

In an effort to organize the plan, I use a work chart. It allows me to note all of the work required for any given canoe. It also keeps track of the time frame for the restoration. Without making notes, I tend to forget when I applied the linseed oil or how long the filler has been drying. By printing a copy of a work chart on a sheet of card stock, I can attach it to the canoe and always have a record of the work on hand.

Planning Your Restoration

On this page, I present a sequence of events for the restoration of your canoe. Actions marked with "#" are done only if required. On the next page, I present a work chart for you to list the work to be done and keep track of the date that each step is completed.

1. Remove the outwales.
2. Remove the stem-bands.
3. Remove the thwarts and seats.
4. Strip the old varnish. #
5. Clean the interior with TSP.
6. Remove the keel. #
7. Remove the old canvas.
8. Remove planks from sheer-line. #
9. Remove planks to expose the ends. #
10. Remove the cant ribs. #
11. Remove the decks. #
12. Stabilize the stem and fill small holes.
13. Rebuild the stem-ends. #
14. Rebuild the inwale-ends. # (Or make and install new inwales. #)
15. Stabilize the rib-tops and fill small holes or gouges before replacing the inwales. #
16. Install new inwales. #
17. Make new decks. #
18. Install the decks and join the stem-end with the inwale-ends.
19. Re-install original planks and cant ribs at the ends.
20. Replace damaged planks or cant ribs. #
21. Repair, rebuild and refinish thwarts and seats. #
22. Re-install thwarts.
23. Make new ribs to replace broken ones. #
24. Bend each replacement rib to fit. #
25. Allow the replacement ribs to dry for about 48 hours. #
26. Remove one broken rib and install the corresponding replacement rib. #
27. Replace broken ribs one at a time to maintain the original shape of the hull. #
28. Rebuild rotted rib-tops. #
29. Re-install original planks around the inwales and replace damaged planks.
30. Replace other broken planks. #
31. Make new keel. #
32. Make new outwales. #
33. Fill small holes and gouges in planks.
34. Sand the hull exterior with 80-grit sandpaper.
35. Vacuum the interior of the canoe and brush the entire canoe.
36. Stain all new wood to match original wood.
37. Apply a mixture of boiled linseed oil and turpentine to the exterior of the canoe.
38. Apply a mixture of boiled linseed oil and turpentine to the interior. #
39. Allow the oil to dry for about two weeks at room temperature.
40. Stretch new canvas on to the canoe and tack it along the inwales and on the seams at each end.
41. Make or obtain canvas filler.
42. Apply canvas filler and rub it smooth.
43. Allow the filler to dry for at least four weeks at room temperature.
44. Sand the filler with 220-grit sandpaper.
45. Install the keel. #
46. Make new stem-bands. #
47. Install the stem-bands.
48. Apply two coats of shellac to all exposed wood in interior and components. #
49. Apply four coats of alkyd enamel waiting 48 hours between coats.
50. Between coats of enamel, apply three coats of spar varnish waiting 48 hours between coats.
51. Apply a coat of carnauba wax to the painted canvas and buff until it shines.
52. Re-install (lower) seats.
53. Install outwales.
54. Install painter rings. #
55. Apply decals to bow deck and/or hull sides. #
56. Allow everything to dry for at least one week at room temperature.
57. Celebrate with a paddle on the lake in your fully restored "old" canoe.

CANOE RESTORATION WORK CHART

Name: _____   Date Started: _____

Canoe Make: _____   Canoe model: _____

Year: _____   Serial No.: _____

Component	Remove	Repair	Make	Install	Apply

Work to be done	?	C	Date	?	C	Date	?	C	Date	?	C	Date	?	C	Date
Old Finish															
Stems															
Decks															
Inwales															
Ribs															
Planks															
Seats															
Thwarts															
Outwales															
Oil/Turp															
Canvas															
Filler															
Keel															
Stem-Bands															
Paint															
Shellac															
Varnish															
Decals															
Other															

? = Check if action is required   **C** = Check when action is completed   **Date** = Completion (mm/dd/yy)

3

Disassembly

At this point, you have a place to work on your canoe and you are starting to collect some basic tools for the job. You have examined your canoe closely and have developed a plan for the project. Now, it is time to get started. In any renovation, whether it be a house or a canoe, the first stage tends to be a little disheartening. It involves a lot of messy work as you tear things apart. However, this process also holds within it a sense of accomplishment and a promise of wonderful things to come.

Stripping Old Varnish

Without a doubt, the most horrible job in the restoration of a wood-canvas canoe is the process of stripping the old varnish from the interior. It is messy, stinky, agonizing work that takes forever and cannot be rushed. As you scrub and scrape, you wonder why you decided to start the project in the first place. The only thing that keeps you going is the fact that, at some point, the job will end.

First, protect yourself from all those nasty chemicals. The commercial products usually contain dichloromethane (commonly used as a propellant in aerosol cans) and methanol (wood alcohol). Sometimes toluene (lacquer thinner) rounds out the mix. Besides long sleeves, long pants and an apron or coveralls, be sure to wear gloves (heavy-duty latex/neoprene), a respirator and eye protection. Have lots of water close by to wash off any stripper that contacts your skin.

(Right) TSP (tri-sodium phosphate) is used to remove any residual chemicals you were unable to scrape out after stripping the varnish. It also cleans original varnish before a new coat of varnish is applied.

If the interior varnish is in good shape – not peeling, cracked or gone altogether – you can simply clean the interior with TSP (tri-sodium phosphate) and rough up the surface of the varnish with fine steel wool. However, in many cases the old varnish has to come off. The best way to remove all of the old varnish is with chemical strippers. Sometimes, the varnish is peeling so much that it comes off with a combination of a paint scraper, coarse steel wool and a lot of elbow grease. I have tried sanders and "sandpaper stripping wheels" powered by a variable-speed drill, but soon gave them up when they removed more wood than varnish. If the old canvas is still attached to your canoe, leave it on until you have finished cleaning and/or stripping the interior. That way, most of the chemicals stay inside the canoe. For those of you who want to strip the old varnish while keeping the original canvas, unfortunately, it can't be done. The old canvas must go.

It is essential to maintain a wetted surface when using varnish strippers. It evaporates quickly, so be sure to use lots of this stuff and do the canoe in small sections (I divide the canoe into quarters). Spread it over the surfaces with a sturdy scrub-brush (natural bristles) and let it sit for about 20 minutes. When it turns dark brown and becomes

(Below) A 1" putty knife gets between the ribs to scrape the dark sludge of chemical stripper out of the canoe's interior.

thick, you know it is working. Use a scrub brush and a scraper to remove the stripper. Any stripper remaining in the canoe can be cleaned out with TSP mixed in a pail of water. Use a scrub brush and a scraper and/or steel wool to remove residual stripper from all the nooks and crannies.

Once the hull interior has dried, I go over the wood again with medium or fine steel wool to remove the last of the TSP and/or chemical stripper residue. To finish the job, use a vacuum cleaner to remove any remaining dust and steel wool fragments.

As much as you want this job to be over as quickly as possible, there is no way to speed it up. It takes time to do the job properly. Sometimes, it even has to be done twice. As always, if you don't do a good job on the foundation work, it simply creates more problems to deal with later.

Removing Old Fasteners

As I approach each new canoe restoration, I brace myself for the inevitable struggle with corroded, damaged or otherwise stubborn screws, nails, bolts and tacks. The degree of difficulty has a lot to do with the type of canoe I'm working on. However, there are some basic tricks of the trade.

The vast majority of wood-canvas canoes were constructed almost exclusively with non-corrosive fasteners. There are exceptions, of course. For example, as the Chestnut Canoe Company attempted to keep the cost of production down in order to compete with the rapidly rising competition from aluminum and fiberglass canoe manufacturers in the 1970's, they used steel fasteners instead of brass, copper or bronze. No matter what sort of fasteners I might find, I tend to haul out every tool I own to wrestle them out of the canoe.

Any of the 2,500 canoe tacks that need to be removed are best tackled with a tack remover available at most hardware stores. Be sure to wear safety glasses while doing this job. Many times the tack will break as you pry it loose, sending half of it towards your eye as though it were shot from a gun. I've lost count of the number of old canoe tacks that have ricocheted off my glasses.

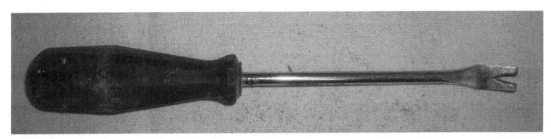

(Top) A simple tack remover is usually available at your local hardware store.

(Bottom) Wear eye protection when removing old canoe tacks. They can snap off and fly at your face without warning.

(Above right and below left) A concave cutter is normally used to prune bonsai trees. It is also perfect for removing difficult fasteners from a wood-canvas canoe.

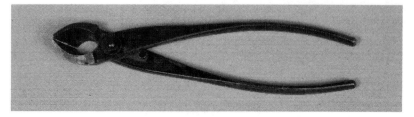

(Right) Vice grips are used to turn out screws that are otherwise impossible to remove.

Sometimes, while removing tacks or the nails attaching rib-tops to inwales, the head breaks off leaving most of it in the wood. To remove them, I use a bonsai concave cutter to dig into the cedar, grab what is left of the tack and rock it out using the rounded face of the cutter as a lever.

The outwales, decks and keel are attached with wood screws. As long as the screws are brass or bronze, they tend to come out without much trouble. Use an awl to clear any debris in the square-drive or slot head to ensure a solid fit with the screw driver. The awl is also useful for removing wood or putty covering outwale screws. Dig out all of the debris before attempting to remove the screw.

For whatever reason, some builders used ferrous (steel) screws. These can usually be removed by heating them first. The heat expands the metal and breaks the corrosion which makes it possible to remove the screw. I insert an old screwdriver in the head of the screw and heat its shaft with a propane torch for a minute or two. The screw then turns out easily.

In some cases, the head is worn enough that it takes a lot of fuss and bother (not to mention holding your tongue just right) to turn the screw at all. If you can get the screw up far enough to grab it with a pair of vise-grips, it can be turned out from there.

(Above left and bottom right) An awl is used to clear debris out of screw heads or remove plugs that cover old screws.

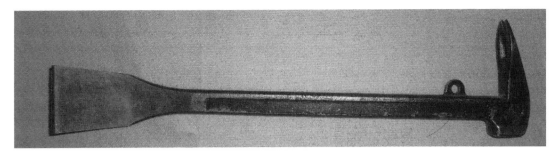

(Top) A catspaw pry bar (also called a restorer's pry bar) and/or a heated screw driver can tease out small screws that are difficult to remove.

When the head is worn beyond the point where a screwdriver can do any good, I heat up the screw and pry it out with a restorer's pry-bar and a heavy hammer. This works for the screws in outwales and stem-bands. When all else fails, I use a large carbide-tipped drill bit and my variable speed drill to drill out the head of the screw. Some builders used top quality naval brass screws to attach outwales. These can often be removed and kept for use again when the outwales are re-installed at the end of the restoration.

Being in British Columbia, I come across a lot of canoes built by Bill Greenwood from 1934 to 1975. They were trimmed entirely with Philippine Mahogany (Luan) and are absolutely gorgeous. Occasionally, I come across a Greenwood canoe where steel screws have corroded into the outwales to the point where I have no choice but to cut the mahogany into a hundred small pieces.

Apparently, Bill Greenwood had a feud with one of his suppliers around 1973. He wanted bronze screws in lots of 1,000 while the supplier would only sell lots of 10,000. The story is that Bill ordered steel screws from another supplier out of pure spite. I suppose he thought he won the war. However, it has created a lot of extra work for canoe restorers a few decades later.

Thwarts and seats are attached to the canoe with carriage bolts or machine screws. They were usually galvanized steel which are often subject to extensive corrosion. Sometimes all that is needed to break the corrosion is a little penetrating oil or a little heat. In other cases, you will have to resort to using a hack saw. A large wooden mallet can then be used to persuade the seat or thwart to disengage from the bolt. The head of the carriage bolt and the remaining shaft corroded into the inwale can usually be loosened with some heat and extracted with a pair of vise grips. I often have to grab the bolt with vice grips and pound them with a heavy hammer to dislodge the bolt. Avoid hitting the bolt directly. It usually only bends the bolt.

(Below right) Galvanized carriage bolts were often screwed into the inwales. Once corroded, a pair of vice grips and a 20-ounce hammer are required to remove them.

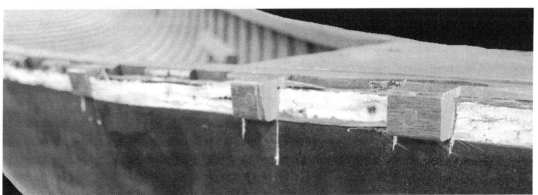

(Bottom) Beautiful mahogany outwales have to be sacrificed because the original builder attached them to the canoe with steel screws.

Removing Fiberglass

So, you have a canoe that someone else covered with fiberglass. By now, the cloth may have delaminated and separated from the wooden hull. In some cases, the resin has cracked. I saw one canoe where some of the tacks had worked loose and rubbed right through the fiberglass.

To remove it, you will need a professional-grade heat gun, a 2" putty knife, a pair of pliers, safety equipment (work gloves, safety glasses, respirator mask, coveralls) and lots of patience. The first step is to move the canoe into a well ventilated work space – preferably outdoors. Then start at an edge of the canoe and apply heat to the resin.

It is important to note that fiberglass resins come in two basic types – polyester and epoxy. If your canoe had fiberglass applied to it in the 1970's, you can bet that polyester resins were used. They tend to become brittle and deteriorate relatively quickly. If you see fiberglass delaminating from a wood canoe, chances are good that you are dealing with a polyester resin. Fortunately, this makes removal comparatively quick and easy. That said, don't get carried away and just rip the cloth off. You could end up tearing sizeable chunks of planking off the canoe at the same time (I speak from first-hand experience).

Epoxy resins hit the market in a big way in the 1980's and are the standard today. They are applied by mixing a hardener with a resin in a two-part formula. What results is a strong, tough plastic that bonds very well to wood. Unfortunately, this means that removal is arduous and painstaking.

As mentioned earlier, start at an edge of the canoe and apply heat to the resin. If you are dealing with epoxy resin, you will probably have to apply the heat for several minutes before the cloth begins to respond to your attempts to lift it with the putty knife. At some point, it softens and the fiberglass cloth can be separated from the canoe. Scrape off any excess resin and move over a few centimeters to a new section and repeat the process. Hold the cloth with a pair of pliers rather than your hand. Even with work gloves on, the pliers prevent nasty encounters with heat and/or sharp edges of fiberglass (again, the voice of experience). If you are dealing with epoxy resin, be prepared to settle into hours of tedious work as the cloth is lifted one square centimeter at a time. It took me 17 hours to remove the fiberglass from a Chestnut Pal that had a double layer of cloth on the bottom.

(Top)Work outside or in a well-ventilated space when removing fiberglass. It is also a good idea to wear a respirator.

(Bottom) Use a putty knife and a heat gun to remove resin still stuck to the planking after the fiberglass is removed.

4

Gunwales, Stems and Decks

(Left) Rotted wood breaks apart into cubes when disturbed. All of this can be repaired and rebuilt.

A s mentioned earlier, if rot is going to be found anywhere, it will be in the ends of the canoe. I will begin this chapter by talking a little bit about rot in general - how it happens, how to repair areas affected by it and how to prevent it in the future once your canoe is restored. I will then take you through the process of repairing areas attacked by wood rot. The task of repairing and/or replacing gunwales, stems and decks often involves having to bend the new wooden components. Therefore, we will examine this process and apply it to the job at hand.

Understanding Wood Rot

Canvas-covered canoes, by their very nature, are subject to rot. The problem is unavoidable and can be dealt with in a number of ways.

Wood rot is caused by a number of fungi (*Serpula lacrimans*, *Poria incrassata* and *Gleophyllum trabeum* are among the most common). These fungi, as with all fungi, grow in environments where plant material (in this case, wood) is allowed to remain moist and warm for extended periods. In this environment your canoe essentially composts. The once solid wood becomes dark brown and crumbly. As you disassembled your canoe, you may have already noticed affected areas break apart into cubes when disturbed.

The fungal spores associated with wood rot are almost always present, but can only grow when certain conditions exist. Generally speaking, fungi need these basic ingredients to grow: 1) food in the form of dead plant material 2) a moist environment 3) no air circulation 4) a warm environment. Any part of your canoe that has been allowed to stay warm and wet becomes a prime environment for fungal growth – in other words, rot heaven.

Preventing rot in the first place is the best course of action in the long run and will be discussed in detail in Chapter 11. At this point, suffice to say, the fungi that cause wood rot will not grow in environments that are dry and cool with lots of air circulation.

End Repairs

Every canoe company had their own stem-end assembly, so the joinery is different for each manufacturer. However, some basic principles apply to every canoe. I will describe the steps required to repair the end of a canoe built by either the Peterborough Canoe Company or the Chestnut Canoe Company. It is a lengthy process that involves:

  1) taking the end apart
  2) splicing in new wood to repair the damaged stem inwale-ends
  3) doing some fancy joinery before putting the end back together again.

(Left) Remove the cant ribs and decks.

Exposing rotted ends

First, use a pencil or permanent-ink marker to identify the planking to be removed. That way, when it is time to reassemble the canoe, the planking can be returned to the correct locations. Use a tack remover to extract the tacks. Then use a utility knife with a sharp blade to cut the planking to the desired lengths.

Remove all of the tacks from the cant ribs. These are located at each end of the canoe on either side. During construction they were inserted after the canoe was removed from the mould. Remove and label them. Now, the fasteners attaching the deck to the inwales are exposed.

Mark the location of the deck on each inwale. In most cases, very little of the inwale-end is removed. Therefore, the original location of the deck is still visible in the original inwale wood. Remove the deck from the canoe. It is usually attached with three bronze or brass screws. At the stern, remove the stern seat to allow the end to be spread open easily.

End Assembly Joinery

Chestnut and Peterborough ends are assembled with rather complex joinery. The inwale-ends meet together at the apex of the deck. The inside faces of the inwale-ends are tight together in a line extending from the center-line of the deck.

The edges of the stem-top trapezoid shape are cut to form a rectangular tenon that sits in a notch between the two inwale-ends. The notch is formed by cutting half of the notch from each inwale-end. The entire end assembly fits tightly, so no fasteners hold the stem-top and inwale-ends together. Everything is stabilized once the hull planking is attached to the stem and inwales.

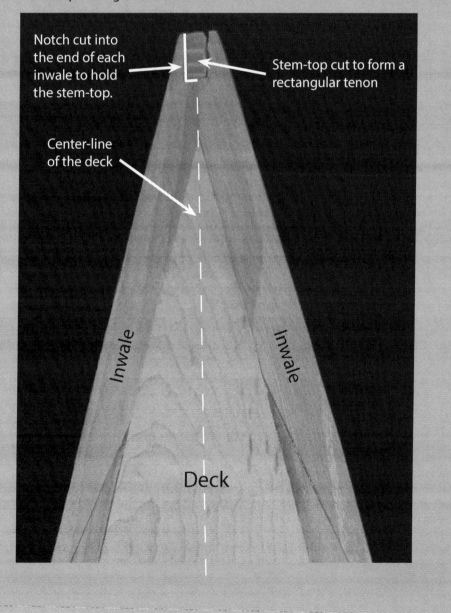

Notch cut into the end of each inwale to hold the stem-top.

Stem-top cut to form a rectangular tenon

Center-line of the deck

Inwale

Inwale

Deck

(Above) A sliding bevel is used throughout the restoration to capture and transfer odd angles in the canoe.

(Top right) Use a sliding bevel and pencil to mark the scarf joint angle on the inwale.

Repairing rotted ends

Spread the inwales apart with a piece of scrap wood to allow for easy access to the end pieces. Use a sliding bevel to mark out a scarf angle in the stem and inwale ends. In order to provide a large surface area for the glued piece of new wood, draw an angle that is at least 6:1. Make sure the line is entirely within solid, unrotted wood.

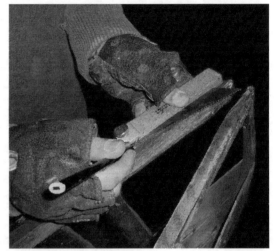

(Bottom right) A saber saw is one of many tools that can be used to cut the rotted inwale-ends and stem-end.

Next, cut off the rotted wood. A number of tools will do the job well. Hand tools such as a Japanese cross-cut saw or a dove-tail saw can be used as well as power tools such as a saber saw or an oscillating saw. Make the cut as straight and plumb as possible. Then use a sander to make sure the cut is both straight and plumb.

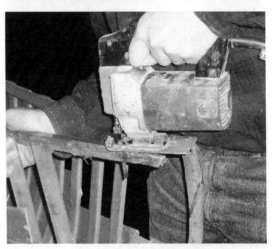

(Bottom) A Japanese cross-cut saw does a great job on tricky joinery cuts.

(Top right) Dry fit the scarf joint and mark the position of the new wood.

Measure the exposed end pieces and mill replacement wood (whatever they are made of – usually ash, oak or fir) to scarf into the ends. Line up the new wood with the cut ends and transfer the scarf angle directly onto the new wood. Cut the scarf angle in the new wood and test it with a dry fit. Sand the cut face of the new wood until you have a perfect fit with the original wood. Use a straight edge to make sure the new wood is perfectly in-line with the original wood. Mark the position of the joint on both the new and old wood.

(Middle right) Glue and clamp the new wood into the original components. Use polyurethane glue and let it cure overnight.

Glue the new wood into place and hold everything with spring clamps while it cures. Use polyurethane glue for these joints and let it sit overnight to cure. Then, sand off the excess glue (80-grit paper on a random-orbital sander) and remove any marks left by the permanent-ink marker.

If the deck has to be replaced with new wood, make the new deck now. This process is described later in the chapter. If the original deck is solid, seal the bare wood on the edges with wood hardener, and let it cure overnight.

(Left) This dovetail saw has 24 tpi (teeth per inch) and a very fine kerf. It is called a razor saw and does a great job on the precise joinery cuts required in end rebuilding.

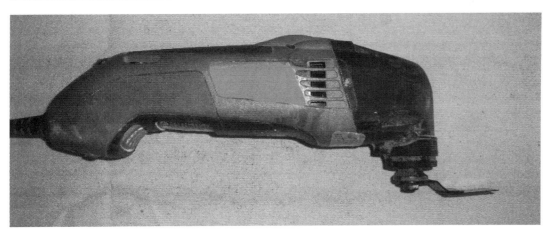

(Bottom) An oscillating saw makes quick work of tricky joinery cuts.

Reassembling the ends

Attach the deck to one inwale at the original location with three #8 – 1½" (38 mm) square drive (Robertson) wood screws. Drill and counter-sink a pilot hole for each screw. A combination bit that drills and countersinks in one operation is useful but not essential.

Securing the screws in the pilot hole can generate a fair amount of heat as the screw works into the hardwood deck. This can weaken the screw and cause it to break. Avoid this by spraying a little penetrating oil into the pilot hole before securing the screw. Use a manual screwdriver to ensure a gentle touch as you drive the screw tight.

(Above) The deck is attached to the inwale with three silicon bronze wood screws. Use a combination bit (top) to drill and countersink pilot holes.

(Left) Find the centre of the deck at the base and extend the centre-line past the apex of the deck onto the new inwale.

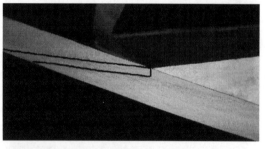

Find the centre line of the deck and extend the line onto the new inwale wood. Then, mark a line parallel to the centre line about 1/8" (3 mm) away that will become a notch in the end of the new inwale.

(Left) Once the new inwale material is cut along the centre-line, replace the deck and mark the location of the inwale on the stem-top.

Mark the position of the deck in the new in-wale material. Then, remove the deck. Cut the new inwale along the centre line being careful not to cut over the line. Cut outside the line and remove the rest of the wood down to the line with a wood rasp. Mark the top and bottom of the inwale on the new stem wood. Mark the outside and inside of the stem onto the new inwale wood. As you do this, stand at the end of the canoe and sight down the centre. When the stem is lined up with the centre-line of the canoe, mark its position along the new inwale.

(Bottom) A wood rasp cleans up rough cuts in joinery.

(Top right) Mark the dimensions of the tenon to be cut in the stem-top.

Trim the new stem-top wood about 1" (2.5 cm) above the new inwale. Then, mark the tenon in the stem-top.

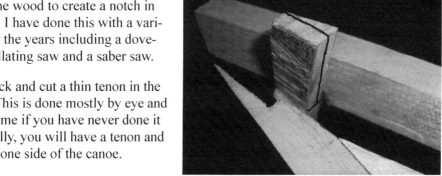

(Right) The notch is cut in one inwale-end and the tenon is cut on one side of the stem-top.

Cut and shape the wood to create a notch in the new inwale. I have done this with a variety of tools over the years including a dovetail saw, an oscillating saw and a saber saw.

Re-attach the deck and cut a thin tenon in the new stem-top. This is done mostly by eye and will take some time if you have never done it before. Eventually, you will have a tenon and notch carved on one side of the canoe.

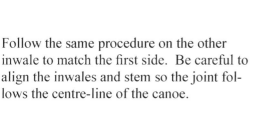

(Right) The notches are cut in both inwales and the tenon is cut in the stem-top.

Follow the same procedure on the other inwale to match the first side. Be careful to align the inwales and stem so the joint follows the centre-line of the canoe.

(Bottom right) The end is assembled and ready to be trimmed and sanded.

Clamp both inwales to the deck and attach the second side with three more screws. Again, it will take some time to create a flush joint at the stem-end. Take your time and use a rasp to shape the joint until it fits.

(Top right) Clamp the end assembly together and use a screwdrive to drive the silicon bronze wood screws.

Secure the inwales to the deck with 1-1/2" (38 mm) #8 silicon bronze wood screws. As before, use penetrating oil to reduce heat build-up in the screws and drive them manually with a screwdriver.

(Right) Trim the excess wood from the inwale-ends and stem-top.

Once assembled, trim the excess wood from the inwale-ends and the stem-top. Then sand the entire assembly to create a fair surface between the outside edge of the inwale and the outside edge of the stem.

(Right) Sand the new end assembly smooth.

Sand the deck and inwale assembly to create a very smooth surface that people will enjoy touching. Work in steps from 120-grit to 220-grit. Wet the top surface of the deck and let it dry (usually about an hour). This lifts the grain and creates a rough surface that was previously smooth. Now, turn to hand sanding in steps from 320-grit to 600-grit. The results are spectacular as the hardwood deck is polished to a silky-smooth finish.

(Bottom right) New wood is stained to match the original wood.

Finally, stain the new wood to match the original wood in the end of the canoe.

New Decks

Making a replica of the original deck is usually a fairly straightforward task. The deck is most often no more than a triangular piece of 4/4 hardwood in the neighbourhood of 12" (30 cm) long and 5" (13 cm) wide at the base. Some decks are extremely complicated (involving steam-bending and fancy joinery). If you are faced with that kind of challenge, talk to the folks at the Canadian Canoe Museum or the Wooden Canoe Heritage Association. For now, let's look at a basic deck.

Select your wood and use the original decks as templates for the replicas. Start by measuring the thickness of the deck with a pair of calipers. Some decks were crowned slightly, so make sure you measure the maximum thickness. Run the board through a thickness planer until you have what you want. If you don't happen to have a thickness planer (or a friend with one), be prepared to do a lot of sanding once the new deck is installed.

Use a permanent-ink marker to mark the basic outline. Draw the lines slightly oversize. The goal is to end up with exact copies of the originals, so start big and work your way down. Many decks are bevelled on the side (typically four or five degrees) to fit the contour of the canoe at the ends.

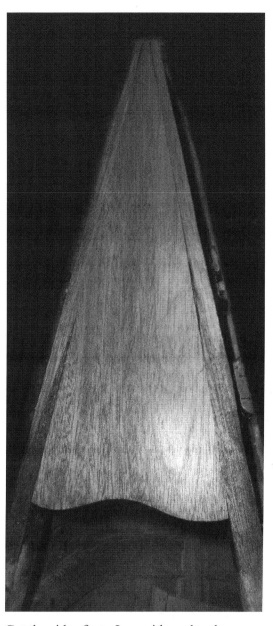

(Right) The recurve deck design and tapered inwales (all in mahogany) help identify this as a Greenwood canoe.

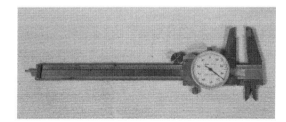

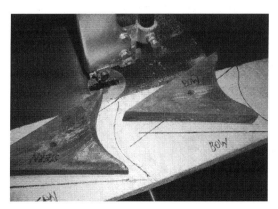

(Top left) Calipers measure the thickness of original components and ensure an exact match in new components.

Cut the sides first. I use either a band saw or a table saw for these cuts. Sand the sides smooth and straight. Check your new decks against the originals until they are exactly the same. Then, cut the base contour. This is typically different for every canoe company. The contour can be concave, convex, recurve – to name a few.

You can bring your own creativity into the final design of the decks. However, bear in mind that one of the key identifying components of your canoe is the deck design. So, if you want people to recognize it as being from a specific company, keep the deck design as close to the original as possible.

(Bottom left) Original decks are used as templates for exact replicas in new wood. A band saw is a useful tool for cutting the curves in new deck material.

CANOE DECK DESIGNS

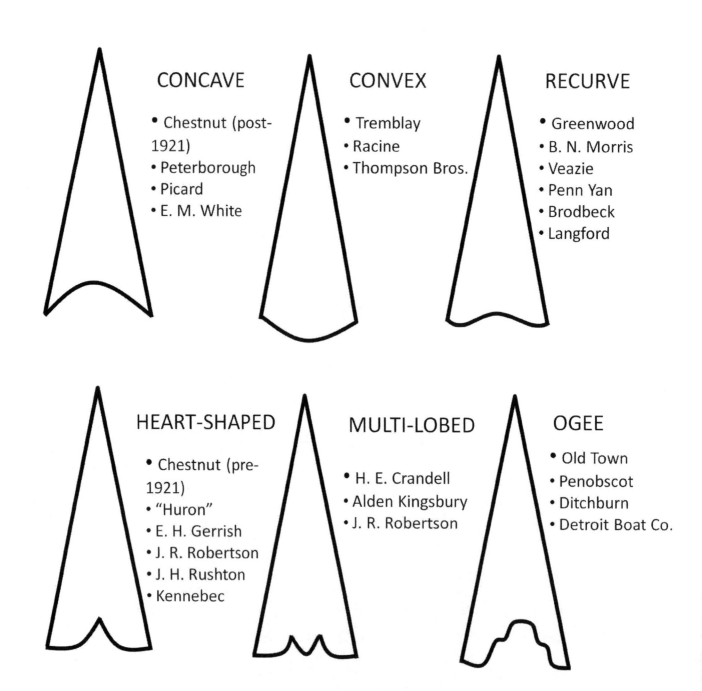

CONCAVE

- Chestnut (post-1921)
- Peterborough
- Picard
- E. M. White

CONVEX

- Tremblay
- Racine
- Thompson Bros.

RECURVE

- Greenwood
- B. N. Morris
- Veazie
- Penn Yan
- Brodbeck
- Langford

HEART-SHAPED

- Chestnut (pre-1921)
- "Huron"
- E. H. Gerrish
- J. R. Robertson
- J. H. Rushton
- Kennebec

MULTI-LOBED

- H. E. Crandell
- Alden Kingsbury
- J. R. Robertson

OGEE

- Old Town
- Penobscot
- Ditchburn
- Detroit Boat Co.

New Stems

Most of the time, the stems of your canoe are in good shape – except for the stem-top. Sometimes, they are completely rotted and/ or broken and need to be replaced. A canoe stem is typically made from one solid piece of hardwood (normally either white oak or white ash). Many canoe restorers choose to laminate a number of thin strips, build them up over a form and glue them together to create the required thickness (typically 3/4" or 19 mm). However, if you are looking for authenticity, you will be bending wood.

Bending wood

The idea of bending a chunk of white ash that is 19mm thick (3/4") tends to scare a lot of people away from the task. However, once you know the basic principles behind the process, it is less frightening.

Wood fibers are made up of millions of cells that have an exterior wall made of cellulose. This tough, strong cell wall cannot be bent or stretched. When you bend wood, you are not bending the individual cells. Instead, it is the space between the cells that changes. Much of this space is filled with lignin – a complex organic polymer – which acts as a glue to hold the cells together to form what we recognize as wood. When wood bends, the space between the cells is either compressed

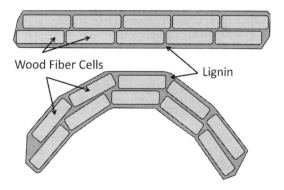

Wood Fiber Cells

Lignin

or lengthened. In order for this to happen, the lignin must be heated until it changes from a solid to a liquid. Then, the cells can move into a new shape. When the wood cools, the lignin solidifies again to hold the new shape. However, we cannot heat the lignin directly without burning the wood. Therefore, we must surround the lignin with hot water. When the internal temperature of the wood reaches 200°F or 93°C, the lignin liquifies and allows the wood to bend.

First Nations builders in North America soaked white cedar ribs in the lake for a couple of days, then poured boiling water over the area they wanted to bend. This worked very well for relatively thin components in the canoe. However, when it came to bending the wood for the stems, they had to bend a collection of thin strips and build them up into a thicker component.

(Top) The individual cells in wood fiber do not bend or stretch. Water and heat liquifies the lignin that holds wood fibers together. The wood can then be bent into a new shape. When the lignin cools, the wood retains its new shape.

(Bottom) A bending form for hardwood components is a basic dowel and wedge system. A metal backing strip and clamps at each end of the wood creates longitudinal compression to help prevent the wood from breaking.

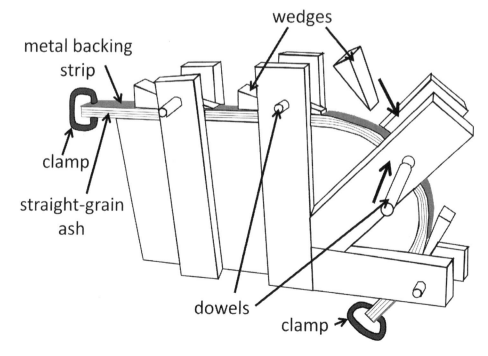

metal backing strip

wedges

clamp

straight-grain ash

dowels

clamp

In 1856, Michael Thonet, a Viennese cabinet-maker, experimented with wood bending. He ran into the same problem encountered by the First Nations canoe builders. As a thicker piece of wood bends, the fibers on the outside of the bend tend to tear or break while the fibers on the inside of the bend remain intact. Thonet clamped a thin metal strap over the outside surface of the piece he was about to bend. As he bent the wood onto a form, the metal strap held the outside fibers to the same length as the inside fibers. This "longitudinal compression" is the key to bending a solid piece of white ash over a form to create the canoe stem.

Building a form

For new stems, you must construct and use a custom-built form to replicate the shape of the originals. I'm sure there are as many types of steam-bending forms as there are canoe builders. Here is the system I use.

Take the shape of the form directly from the original stem by tracing the inside curve of the stem onto a piece of cardboard held against the end of the canoe. Transfer it to a piece of ¾" (19 mm) plywood. The curve in the form must be greater than the final curve desired in order to compensate for a certain amount of "spring-back" in the new wood once it has been bent and dried. I usually add about 2" (5 cm) more curve at one end of the form. Extend the lines of the form about 6" (15 cm) past the required length at both ends. This provides room for clamping stations on the form and produces a stem piece with extra length at each end to be trimmed

later. Laminte three pieces of 3/4" (19mm) plywood together and cut the shape of the form. This creates a form 2.25" (57 mm) wide. It provides enough room for a piece of stem stock 2" (51 mm) wide. Once bent, the stock will be cut into two pieces, each of which will be 7/8" (22 mm) wide.

Cut a number of plywood strips 2½" (63 mm) wide. These will be the braces for the holding points along the length of the form. For a stem form, I use four or five holding points.

Each holding point consists of a dowel and wedge system held in the braces. A ¾" (19 mm) hardwood dowel is placed in a 7/8" (22 mm) hole in each set of braces. The dowel is located so that the 3/4" (22 mm) high stem plus a 1/16" (2 mm) backing strip fit between the top of the form and the dowel. There must also be enough room to allow a hardwood wedge to fit between the stem and the dowel. Each brace piece extends at least 3¼" (83 mm) beyond the top edge of the form. The centre point for a 7/8" (22 mm) hole is placed about 1.5" (38 mm) above the top of the form. Attach each of the braces on one side of the bending form at their intended locations using 2" (5 cm) deck screws.

Now, flip the form over and place the braces in their intended positions. Insert the dowel into the holes and make sure that the dowel fits properly. It should fit easily into the holes on each side of the form and be located with enough space to accommodate the stem, backing strip and wedge.

(Left) Use a permanent-ink marker to transfer the inside curve of the original stem onto a piece of cardboard. Add about 2" (5 cm) of curve to each end of the stem profile. This forms the template for the bending forms that are cut from sheets of plywood.

(Right) A form is built to make new stems for a "Huron" canoe. The curve in the form is about 2" (5 cm) tighter at each end to allow for spring-back when the new wood is released from the form.

Steam bending

At this point, we have a bending form and a basic understanding of the process. Now, select the piece of white ash that is to become the new stems. The edge grain will be on the sides of the stem and must be as straight as possible. Any run-out will result in a break – even with the backing strap.

Cut the piece 2" (51 mm) wide and run it through a thickness planer until it is 3/4" (19 mm) thick. The piece will be long enough to make the stem plus extra length as a lever arm to make bending less strenuous. I usually use a piece about 72" (183 cm) long.

Normally, there is not enough water in the wood to heat the lignin effectively. There is a fine balance when soaking the wood. Not enough and the lignin will not heat properly resulting in wood that breaks. Too much soaking and the wood fibers will collapse on the inside surface of the bend, For a piece of wood 3/4" (22 mm) thick, soak the ash for about 96 hours. If you don't have a lake right outside your workshop, set up a length of ABS pipe capped at one end with a removeable cap at the other.

Once the wood has been soaked, it is heated with steam. The amount of steaming required depends on the thickness of the wood. Stem stock 3/4" (19mm) thick requires about 50 or 60 minutes in the steam box. Again there is a fine balance here. Not enough steaming and the lignin will not liquify; too much steam and the wood dries out resulting in a piece of woody mush.

When the grain runs straight down the full length of the wood, the piece will bend and remain solid.

When the grain is crooked or "runs out", the piece will break when you try to bend it.

A key element in this process is the steam generation itself. It takes a lot of steam to create the heat required to bend the wood. I use a large pot over a propane stove. My steam box (a plywood box with inside dimensions of 12" (30 cm) high, 12" (30 cm) wide and 7' (213 cm) long) sits directly above it with supports on each end to keep everything steady. Each piece of wood in the box must have lots of air around it to allow the steam to heat each piece evenly. A series of dowels in my box creates three shelves.

(Left) A plywood steam-box sits on top of a large pot of boiling water heated by a single burner propane stove. The box is supported on both ends to keep everything steady.

(Right) The original stem is used as a template to make an exact replica.

With the heated wood pliable and ready to bend, remove the wood, attach the backing strap with a spring clamp at both ends, place one end of the wood onto the form at the lowest clamping station and start bending. Apply firm, even pressure. As it bends past each successive clamping station, insert a dowel and wedge and tap the wedge into place. The whole operation is best completed in less than a minute. After that, the wood cools which makes bending more difficult. A minute doesn't seem like a lot of time, but it is ample to get the job done without rushing.

Once the wood is bent onto the form, make sure the wood is securely in place. Give each wedge an extra tap or two. Then, allow the wood to dry for at least 96 hours at room temperature with lots of air circulation.

(Below) While it is possible to install a new stem by yourself, it is much easier when you have a friend's help.

If you succeed the first time through this, I take my hat off to you. There is a substantial learning curve in all of this. However, the

results are worth it. You now have a solid piece of ash you can shape into two new stems for your old canoe.

Shaping and installation

Set the fence on the table saw to the maximum width of the original stems. You will be using both of the original stems as templates throughout the installation process, so keep them handy.

Pair up each of the new stems with each of the original stems and label them so as not to get them mixed up later. As you hold the new bow stem beside the original bow stem, it ought to match almost exactly. Use a pencil to mark the position of each rib notch as well as all of the tapers and bevels in the stem. The tenon in the stem-top will be cut once the stem is installed.

Use a dovetail saw or similar tool to cut the notches. Knock out the waste wood in each notch with a chisel and mallet. To shape the tapers and bevels, I turn a belt sander upside-down and clamp it to my work bench. A 50-grit sandpaper belt makes short work of the shaping required. A light touch is required in all of this; err on the side of "not enough" rather than "too much". When you have an exact replica of the original stem, sand all of the exposed surfaces to 220-grit.

Can you put it back to the way it was originally?

A few years ago, Brian brought his Chestnut Chum (15' Pleasure canoe) into the shop. He had just acquired it from someone who had bought it new in the mid-1960's. Apparently, the original owner wanted to use a small outboard motor with the canoe, so he cut off the stern and installed a small transom. Brian asked me to remove the transom and rebuild the entire end to bring the canoe back to its original shape and construction.

I used the bow as a basic guide and rebuilt the entire stern. It involved making a new stem, pre-bending new pieces for the inwales that were spliced into the originals, making a new deck copied from the bow and bending six new ribs. It took a few attempts to get the correct bend in some of the ribs, but in the end, Brian was hard pressed to tell which end had been rebuilt.

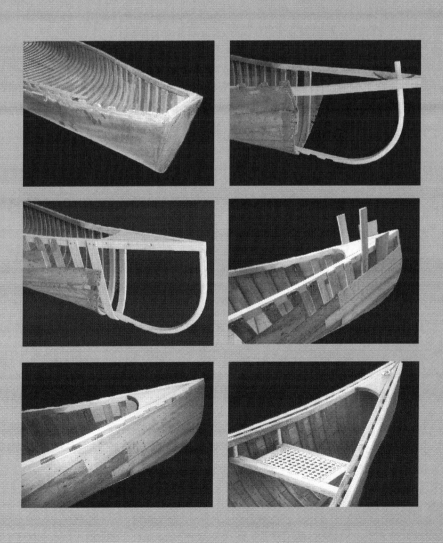

(Right) Use a combination square and a marker to transfer the positions of the seats, thwarts and decks onto the hull of the canoe. This information comes in handy when you want to re-install these components into new inwales.

New Gunwales

The outwales are often rotted and must be replaced with exact replicas of the originals. Sometimes, the inwales are also beyond repair and need to be replaced. This task involves what amounts to taking the entire canoe apart and putting it back together again. The first step is to disassemble the canoe as described in Chapter 3.

The positions of the decks, thwarts and seats will be lost once the inwales are removed, so the first step is to mark those on the hull of the canoe. Place a combination square on the inwale and use a marker to draw a line at right angles to the inwale at each carriage bolt position as well as the location of each deck. Extend the line into the second row of planking because you will be removing the top row.

Now, expose the rib-tops by removing the top row of planks around the entire canoe. Replacing the inwales necessitates opening the ends of the canoe as described earlier in this chapter. As you do this, you'll often discover that the stem-ends need to be repaired. Do this first before continuing with the inwale replacement.

If you expect to have your canoe sitting around for several weeks before the new inwales are installed, secure ratchet straps around the hull to maintain the shape of the canoe. Thread them under the inwales at each thwart and seat position.

(Below) The top row of planks around the entire canoe is removed to expose the rib-tops and facilitate the removal of the original inwales.

Make the new inwales and outwales from wood that matches the originals. This can be white oak, white ash, Douglas fir or mahogany depending on the manufacturer. The edge grain will be showing on the top surface of both the inwales and outwales. Most boards of lumber are "flat sawn" where the edge grain is on the side. To cut the gunwale stock, the first cut is the height of the component. Then, turn the piece ninety degrees to put the edge grain on the top and bottom. The second cut is the final width of the component. Other cuts are usually required to create the final shape of the component.

Even fifty years ago, it was next to impossible to find full length wood for the gunwales. So, cut four pieces from a 10' (3 meter) board for two inwales and do the same for two outwales. Splice two pieces together with a scarf joint to create each inwale and outwale. Make a jig to cut the gunwale scarf joints. The angle of the cut is 12:1.

Sometimes, the sheer-line rises sharply near the ends. If this is the case in your canoe, you will have to pre-bend the gunwales to make them fit. This cannot be done later. Make forms for the gunwales, soak the ends for 48 hours, clamp each piece into the form at the end and pour one cup (250 ml) of boiling water over the piece to heat the wood and allow it to bend easily on to the form. Allow the pieces to dry for at least 48 hours before removing them from the forms. Clamp each piece on to the canoe to line up the bend in the gunwales with the bend in the new piece. Mark the position of each scarf joint, then cut them on the table saw jig.

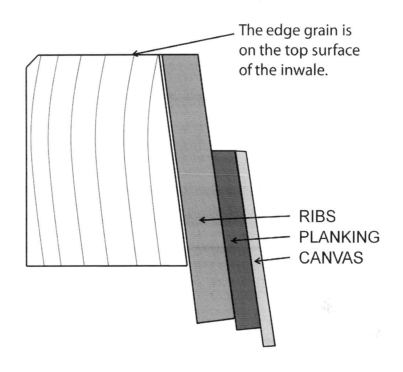

The edge grain is on the top surface of the inwale.

RIBS
PLANKING
CANVAS

(Above) Both inwales and outwales are cut so that the edge grain is on the top surface.

(Right) A jig is made to cut 12:1 scarf joints in new gunwales. Two 10' lengths are joined to create new 19' gunwales.

(Left) Custom-built forms were made to pre-bend new ash gunwales in a Chestnut Pal. This is one of many canoes where the sheer-line rises sharply about 18" from the end.

55

(Top) Polyurethane glue makes a strong waterproof joint in these new ash outwales.

Wet the surfaces of the scarf joints and apply polyurethane glue. Clamp the joints and let them cure overnight. The cured joints are sanded smooth with 80-grit paper and a random-orbital sander.

With the new inwales ready for installation, remove the thwarts and seats as described in Chapter 3. Next, use a few spring clamps to keep the original inwales in position as the old fasteners are removed. Now, use a tack remover and a pair of concave cutters to remove the fasteners from the rib-tops. Be gentle.

Solidify the exposed rib-tops with a wood hardener. Allow the hardener to cure overnight. Then, fill the holes and cracks with two-part epoxy putty.

Once the putty has hardened, sand both the inside and outside surfaces of each rib-top to smooth them out. I usually use an 80-grit sandpaper and a light touch. The combination of a coarse sandpaper and a power sander is aggressive, so be careful to smooth the surfaces without removing a lot of wood.

(Left) Wood hardener is applied to all of the rib-tops around the canoe. Holes and gouges are then filled with two-part epoxy putty.

(Right) Sand the rib-tops smooth after the epoxy putty has hardened.

To install the new inwales, clamp one in place at the centre on one side of the canoe. Make sure the top surface of the inwale is flush with the rib-top. Drill a pilot hole and secure every rib top to the inwale with two 7/8" (22 m) 14-gauge bronze ring-nails. A tack hammer and a clinching iron are used to drive the nails into place. Start in the middle of the canoe on one side and work towards each end. Then, install the other inwale.

Use a random-oribital sander and 80- grit paper to smooth the top and inside surfaces. Work progressively to 220-grit paper to polish those surfaces and round off the inside corners of the inwales. Leave the top edge sharp at the ends to accommodate the decks.

Assemble the ends and stain the new wood to match the original wood in the canoe.

(Above) A dolly is used as backing while a bronze ring nail is hammered into a rib-top to attach it to a new inwale.

(Below) Pre-bending the new inwales for this Chestnut Bobs Special was essential in order to achieve a proper fit along the sheer-line that turns up sharply at the ends.

Away from the family for twenty years

As a kid, Dan practically grew up in his family's 17' Chestnut Prospector. It was a major part of his life until his father sold the canoe without consulting the rest of the family. About twenty years later, Dan had a chance encounter with the man who had bought the canoe. The first question Dan asked was, "Do you still have the canoe?" When the man said yes, Dan bought the canoe in less time than it took to take out his cheque book.

As Dan and I looked at the canoe, it was clear that many things had changed since it was part of the family. Repairs had been made in a make-shift manner and the canvas was a dark forest green instead of the original light green. But the biggest difference was the shape of the hull. The canoe had been stored on the concrete floor of the previous owner's garage – leaning up against a wall with its full weight resting on the gunwales. After many years in this position, the canoe was noticeably flat on the starboard side.

The only way to restore the fair lines of the canoe was to install new gunwales. Dan also asked for the original light green colour. There was a tearful family reunion when the canoe was completed.

Before   **After**

5
Ribs and Planks

A pile of broken ribs as well as a few failed attempts at new ribs are all from one canoe.

Y ou may have started restoring your canoe with the idea of simply putting on a new canvas and adding a coat or two of fresh varnish to the interior. But once the old canvas is off, you might as well do a few repairs while you are at it. In most cases, this means repairing some damaged rib-tops and replacing a couple of broken ribs. Before long you have replaced a dozen ribs and almost half of the planks. Perhaps a question comes to mind about now: "What was I thinking?"

New Ribs

During the assessment of your canoe, it is common to find at least a couple of broken ribs. Fortunately, the canoe hull is a study in pure elegance. The hull tapers toward each end in a graceful, flowing curve. This taper is critical for the canoe restorer. It allows the existing hull to be used as the mould for replacement ribs. You will bend new wood over the outside of the hull to create exact replicas of broken ribs located on the inside.

(Top) A new rib bent over the outside of the hull (Position A) is exactly the same size and shape as the broken rib on the inside of the hull (Position B).

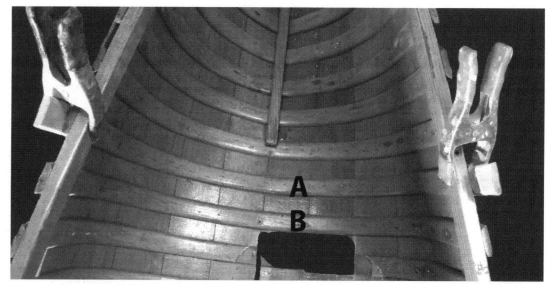

(Bottom) A tapered notch in a piece of plywood forms a simple jig for the table saw. It tapers the 2-3/8" "regular" Chestnut canoe ribs to 1-1/2" over a length of about 16".

Part of the genius in the design of these canoes is the fact that the ribs are spaced along the tapered hull so that a new piece of cedar bent directly on top of one rib results in the creation of a new rib that is exactly the same dimension as the rib next to it on the inside of the canoe.

I don't recommend that you take your canoe apart completely, but if you did, you would find that most of the ribs nest together one inside the next like a set of Russian matryoshka dolls. This means that when you come across a broken rib, its replacement can usually be made by bending new cedar directly over the rib next to it (the next smaller rib). Sometimes, as we saw in the story of Brian's canoe in Chapter 4, the original hull shape is crushed or missing altogether. However, most canoes are symmetrical. Both ends are exactly the same shape. Therefore, it is almost always possible to find a rib that can be used as a mould for a replacement rib.

Preparing new rib stock can be as simple as cutting clear, straight-grained cedar to the appropriate width and thickness, or it can involve many chamfers and tapers. The "regular" ribs in many Chestnut canoes (2-3/8" or 60 mm wide) are tapered on one side. Other builders tapered the ribs on both sides. Whatever the design of the rib, it is important to duplicate the shape of the original. The goal is to make repairs that don't look like repairs. Therefore, take the time to duplicate tapers with specialized jigs.

The edges of the ribs are rarely right angles, so use a sliding bevel to transfer the chamfer angles into the new wood.

Once the new rib stock is prepared, the wood is soaked for about 48 hours and then steamed for about 50 minutes.

Before bending the new rib, prepare the canoe by turning it upside-down on the cradles. Mark the position for bending the rib on the hull with a permanent-ink marker. Place a weight (I use an old 12-volt car battery) on the hull next to the bending position. Place a couple of spring clamps on the hull next to the bending position. Once the rib is removed from the steambox, you will not want to be wasting time looking for tools.

Remove the rib from the steam box and clamp it at the inwale on one side of the canoe. Be sure that at least one inch (25 mm) of the rib extends past the top edge of the inwale. Bend the rib until it lays flat against the bottom of the canoe. Place the weight on the rib to hold it in position. Move around to the other side of the canoe (or have another person ready to bend the rib on that side). Complete the bend and clamp the rib.

Let the rib dry for at least two days. Mark the centre-line on the new rib. Also mark an arrow on the rib pointing toward the nearest end of the canoe. These orientation marks allow for easy installation.

(Bottom) You have about 30 second to bend the steamed rib over the canoe hull. An old 12-volt car battery holds the rib in place while you move from one side of the canoe to the other.

(Top) Use a tack remover to remove all of the tacks holding the broken rib to the planks. Be sure to wear safety glasses.

Installing New Ribs

The replacement process starts on the outside of the hull with a tack remover to remove a section of plank to expose the rib-top on either side. It is not necessary to remove a long length of planking. Just expose the rib-tops of the broken ribs. Now, remove all of the tacks driven through the planking to hold the broken rib in place. Next, use a Japanese cross-cut saw (or similar cross-cut tool) to cut the broken rib just below the inwale on both sides of the canoe. Use a concave cutter to remove the remaining pieces of rib-top as well as the nails driven into the inwales to hold the rib-tops in place. Normally, the rib simply falls out once all of the fasteners are removed. However, sometimes a little persuasion is required.

(Bottom) Remove the plank at the sheer-line to expose the top of the broken rib. Cut the broken rib below the inwale. Use concave cutters to expose and remove old nails from the inwale.

62

Use medium steel wool to clean the hull in the area where the rib was. Remove the replacement rib from the outside of the hull. Before placing it in the canoe, check the arrow and make sure it is pointing toward the nearest end of the canoe. Insert the new rib and hold it in place with spring clamps at the inwales. Adjust the fit of the rib until it sits fair with the ribs on either side. This is especially noticeable and critical at the chine. You may want to use a long section of scrap wood against the outside of the hull to make sure it maintains a fair line with the rest of the hull. A helper makes this job much easier. One person can hold the rib in place while the other person checks for a fair hull. Use clamps at the inwales to hold the final position. Then, one person holds the clinching iron while the other drives

the tacks with a cobbler's hammer. Start at the chine to establish a good fit. Before the tacks are hammered and clinched, make sure the new rib is positioned in exactly the same place as the original.

Once all the tacks are clinched, pre-drill two holes in each rib-top and attach it to the inwale with two 14-gauge silicon bronze ring nails. Drive the nails with the cobbler's hammer while the clinching iron is used to provide a solid backing on the inwale. Use a cross-cut saw to trim the rib-tops flush with the top surface of the inwales. Cut about halfway through on one side of the rib, then complete the cut by cutting from the other side. This prevents the saw from tearing away a piece of the rib-top at the edge. Sand the rib-tops smooth with 120-grit sandpaper and a random-orbital sander.

(Top left) Hammer tacks through the plank from the outside and clinch them tight with a clinching iron. Start at the chine and check for fair lines in the hull as you go.

(Top right) Cut the rib-top flush with the inwale. A Japanese cross-cut saw does a great job.

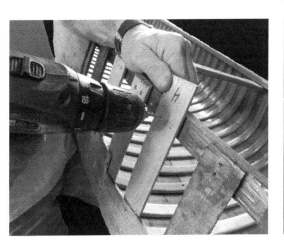

(Bottom left) Pre-drill pilot holes in the rib -top.

(Bottom right) Drive 7/8" bronze ring nails into the rib-top to attach it to the inwale. Use a clinching iron as backing.

(Above) Cut off the rotted rib-top (left), carve a long scarf angle into the original rib (middle) and glue a new rib-top onto the original rib with water-based waterproof glue (right).

(Left) Glue and clamp a cracked rib-top.

Rib-Top Repairs

You may come across some ribs that are perfectly good except for damage to the rib-top. Rather than replacing the entire rib, it is possible to repair the rib-top.

If the damage is minor (usually just a split in the rib-top), it can be glued together with water-based waterproof (resorcinol) glue, clamped overnight and sanded smooth the next day.

If the damage to the rib-top is substantial (usually involving rot in the area), start by removing the planks along the sheer-line as well as enough of the other planks to expose about 4" (10 cm) below the rib top damage. Identify each plank as it comes off and set it aside to be re-installed later.

Prepare new cedar to replace the damaged rib-tops. Sometimes the rib-tops are tapered, so make sure each replacement piece is cut and shaped to match the original wood.

(Top) An angle grinder set up with a 24-grit sanding disk is a versatile carving tool for canoe restoration.

Cut the rotted top off the rib with a Japanese cross-cut saw and remove any old fasteners from the inwale.

Next, create a scarf angle in the original rib with a rasp or a 4" angle grinder set up with a 24-grit sandpaper disc. The power-tool makes quick work of the job – perhaps too quick. Pay careful attention and use a light touch.

Line up the new wood with the original rib and transfer the location of the matching scarf. Then, cut the new wood to length and make the scarf to fit.

Glue the new wood to the original rib with resorcinol glue and clamp it in place with spring clamps overnight.

The repaired rib-top is fairly rough at first. However, a quick sanding evens out the joint and creates a clean repair.

Attach the rib-top to the inwale as described in the previous section and trim it flush with the top of the inwale.

When faced with rib-top repairs next to each other, do them on alternate days to avoid clamping difficulties. It usually takes a few days to repair all of the damage.

(Bottom left) a newly glued rib-top repair looks rough at first.

(Bottom right) A rib-top repair looks great once it is sanded smooth.

Out of a snowbank and back on the water

It was mid-January when I arrived at Gerald's house to pick up his 17' Greenwood canoe and bring it to my shop. He said it would only take a minute to dig the canoe out of the snowbank. We found it frozen into ice all around the gunwales. It took about an hour of hacking at the ice to release the canoe.

A few months later, I grabbed the centre thwart to pick up the canoe. As I pulled, the entire inwale ripped away. Apparently, after sitting in the snow for several months, almost all of the rib-tops had rotted. After repairing 102 rib-tops, the canoe was as good as new.

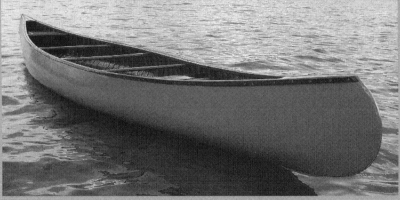

New Planks

One of the most challenging aspects of planking your canoe is making the planks. They are very thin (usually about 5/32" or 4 mm thick) and are best done by cutting a board to about 3/8" or 10 mm and using a thickness plane to shave it down from there. After several years of fussing with this for every canoe that came into the shop, I enlisted a local sawyer to mill an entire log for me. The only thing I do now is cut the rough-edged boards to the desired width for any given canoe. This is often the best way to go since many canoes have at least two different plank widths in addition to tapered planks at the chine.

I'll approach the discussion of new plank installation first by describing how to install a simple straight piece typically found on the bottom of the canoe. I'll then describe the process in increasing levels of complexity at the ends, sheer-line and chine.

Approach the task by installing planks in the following order: 1) the bottom 2) the sheer-line 3) the chine 4) the ends.

Bottom Planks

Any planks that need to be replaced on the bottom of the canoe can be done first. These are basic planks that allow you to practise the procedure without any complications.

Identify the sections of plank to be removed and mark them with a permanent-ink marker. To maintain strength in the hull, make sure replacement sections of planking span at least two ribs. The butt-joints will be on either side of the span, so you will be removing tacks from at least four ribs. If the replacement section is located within two ribs of an original butt-joint, I tend to replace the entire piece to avoid short, weaker sections of planking in the canoe.

Use a fresh blade in a utility knife to cut the old planks. Remove the damaged pieces and clean the exposed sections of rib with medium steel wool. The cut plank-ends must leave enough rib on either side of the cut to allow four tacks to be driven into each butt-end. When an adjacent plank is also removed, make sure that the cuts are staggered.

(Top left) Capture the butt-joint angle with a sliding bevel.

(Top right) Use a pencil to transfer the butt-joint angle onto a new piece of cedar planking.

Assuming you have planking cut to the required width and thickness to match the existing planks, the next step is to determine the angle of one of the butt-joints. Capture the angle with a sliding bevel. Then, transfer the angle to the new plank. Cut the plank at the desired angle (I use either a mitre saw or a Japanese cross-cut saw).

Set the new plank into position at the butt-joint you just created and mark the location of the butt-joint at the other end. Before fitting the new plank, mark the location of the second butt-joint on the plank below the joint. This allows you to locate the position of the butt-joint when the new plank is in place. Mark that position on the new plank. Then, capture the second butt-joint angle and transfer it to the new plank just as you did for the first angle.

When you cut the plank to the final length, do not worry about cutting slightly on the short side. Small gaps in the butt-joints are typical. These will be filled later with wood filler. However, avoid cutting the plank too short and not having enough planking at both ends to afford strong, solid joints.

Secure the plank with four tacks on each end for a total of eight tacks at each butt-joint. The rest of the plank is secured to each rib with three tacks. Copy the tacking pattern used by the original builder. Some builders used planking about 4" (10 cm) wide and secured it with four tacks at each rib.

(Bottom right) Attach a new plank onto the canoe with four tacks at the butt-joint and three tacks at each rib along its length.

(Bottom left) Use a pencil to mark the location of the second butt-joint. Then, capture the angle and transfer it to the plank at the marked location.

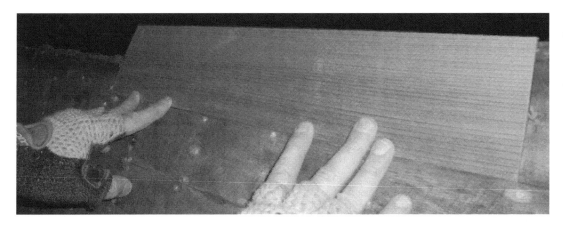

(Top) Set a new sheer-line plank in place and attach it with a number of tacks. Much of the plank extends above the rib-tops. (Photo by Brittany Merry)

Sheer-Line Planks

Planking along the sheer-line is often rotted. Many (if not most) of them must be replaced. These planks require a custom fit, so start by capturing the angle with the sliding bevel. The new plank is now secured with some tacks. In many cases, much of the plank will extend above the sheer-line.

Trim it flush to the rib-tops with a draw-knife or utility knife. In most canoes, the planking is trimmed ½" below the rib-tops to allow the outwales to fit flush with the rib-tops. Mark this trim-line with the sheer-line gauge and cut it with a utility knife. Complete the installation of the piece with a series of tacks to secure the plank to the inwale.

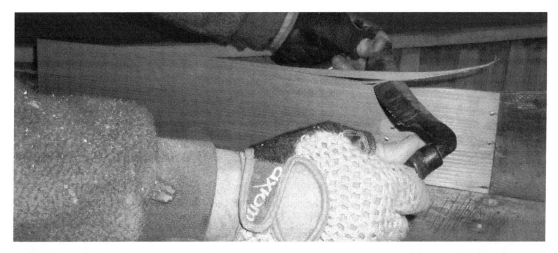

(Middle) Use a draw knife to trim the new plank flush with the rib-tops. (Photo by Brittany Merry)

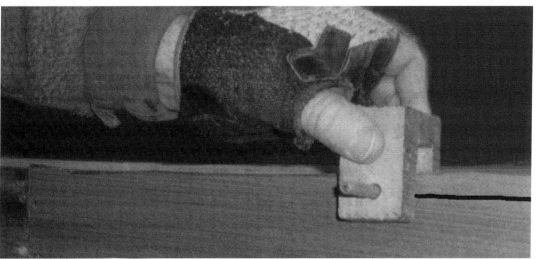

(Bottom) Use a sheer-line gauge to mark the top of the plank which is often 1/2" (13 mm) below the rib-tops. (Photo by Brittany Merry.)

(Top) A damaged plank in the chine of the canoe is removed.

Chine Planks

Many of the planks in the chine are tapered to fit the curves of the hull. Replacing them requires precise measurement, tapering, bending and fitting. The first time I tackled this job, I used nothing more than a steel rule, a pencil and a utility knife. After a lot of fussing, I was able to transfer the taper of the opening onto the new plank. However, with the help of a planking gauge, the job has become relatively quick and hassle-free.

Start with a plank wide enough to fit the widest section of the chine plank. Fit it for length as described earlier and use a planking gauge to transfer the shape of the opening onto the new plank.

Join the marks on the new plank with a straight edge and then do a rough cut with a utility knife. Cut the plank over-size to allow for final fitting. Then, trim the tapered edge of the new plank with a small plane until it fits. Since the chine is curved and the plank is not, most of this fitting is estimated and won't be finalized until the plank is soaked, heated and bent into its final position.

Soak the fitted plank for 20-30 minutes. Then, heat it with boiling water. The hot plank will bend to fit the opening. It is best to have one person hold the plank in position while a second person drives tacks and clinches them tight. Keep a utility knife close to do extra trimming as required.

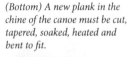

(Bottom) A new plank in the chine of the canoe must be cut, tapered, soaked, heated and bent to fit.

End Planks

At the ends of the canoe, the installation of new planks requires tapering and bending as well as attachment directly to the stem. Some of the original planks can be re-installed with new tacks. Other planks are replaced with the techniques described earlier. Secure the planks to the stem with 5/8" (16 mm) tacks. Sometimes, pre-drilling may be required. Once installed, cut the plank flush with the stem. I use an electric sabre saw for this while others use a coping saw.

The compound curves at the ends often produce wedge-shaped gaps between some of the planks. Some builders filled these with specially fitted pieces. You can either replicate this or custom-fit a wide plank to fit the flared opening. The easiest way to measure and mark this piece is with a planking gauge.

The planks that run from the bottom of the canoe to the stem need to be soaked, heated and bent to fit. These planks twist ninety degrees from the horizontal bottom to the vertical stem. An extra set of hands is very useful for this operation. Attach the plank to

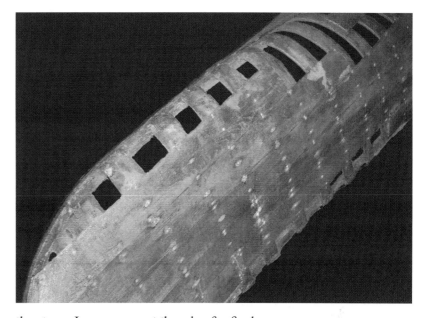

(Above) Damaged planks in the bottom of the canoe at the end are removed.

the stem. Leave room at the edge for final shaping. Once installed, use a draw knife to shave the edges of the plank to fit the rounded contour of the stem.

Before the ends are planked at the sheerline, re-install the cant-ribs (if it was removed to rebuild the end) and secure them with 5/8" (16 mm) tacks.

(Bottom) A new plank on the bottom of the canoe at the end must be soaked and heated to allow it to twist from a horizontal orientation at one end to a vertical orientation at the other end.

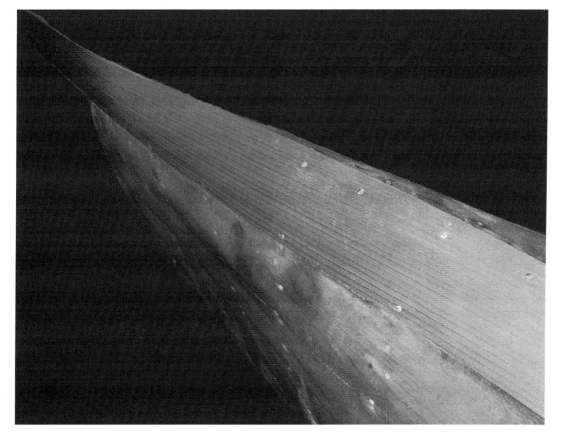

6
Seats and Thwarts

Rawhide "babiche" lacing on hardwood frames is part of a uniquely Canadian canoe.

Most of the time, you will be removing the thwarts and seats from your canoe, refinishing and re-installing them with new non-corrosive hardware. Sometimes, the original hand-woven cane is beyond repair, or mice have eaten the rawhide in your original babiche seats. Perhaps this is a canoe you found in a neighbour's shed and since it is now your canoe, you want it to reflect your style and interest. The seats and thwarts are at the heart of your canoe's style and character. They are not just functional components; they can give your canoe real class. Following the descriptions of how to create seats is a presentation of how to carve a hardwood portage yoke.

Hand-Woven Cane Seats

Usually, the frames for hand-woven cane seats in an old wood-canvas canoe are structurally sound and only require refinishing and re-caning. However, sometimes you may want to replace the original slat seats with cane seats. In this case, the frames must be built from scratch. In Chestnut and Peterborough canoes (and probably others I am less familiar with), the original frames were joined with 3/16" (5 mm) dowel. Some people choose to use the same joint when replicating the seat frames. I use a mortise and tenon joint to create a stronger frame.

Hand-Woven Seat Frame

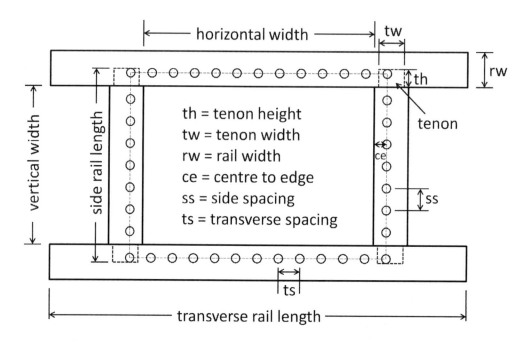

Hand-Woven Seat Frame Dimensions

Component	Position	Imperial	Metric
Transverse rail	Bow	32.00"	81.0 cm
(length)	Stern	20.00"	51.0 cm
Side rail	Bow	8.00"	20.0 cm
(length)	Stern	8.00"	20.0 cm
Horizontal width	Bow	11.25"	28.6 cm
(internal)	Stern	9.25"	23.5 cm
Vertical width	Bow	6.50"	16.5 cm
(internal)	Stern	6.50"	16.5 cm
Seat frame stock	Width	1.50"	38.0 mm
	Thickness	3/4"	19.0 mm
Tenon	Width	1-1/8"	29.0 mm
	Height	3/4"	19.0 mm
	Thickness	3/8"	9.5 mm
Holes	Diameter	3/16"	4.8 mm
Centre of hole to	inside edge	1/2"	13 mm
Hole	Transverse	3/4"	19 mm
Spacing	Side	1.00"	25 mm
Transverse Holes	Bow	17	
(number)	Stern	13	
Side Holes	Bow	7	
(number)	Stern	7	

(Top left) An oscillating saw or razor saw cuts along the bottom edge of the tenons. This helps prevent tear out on the table saw.

(Top right) The tenons on the side pieces are cut with a dado blade on a table saw equipped with a tenon jig.

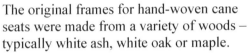

The original frames for hand-woven cane seats were made from a variety of woods – typically white ash, white oak or maple.

Cut the tenons on the side rails with a set of dado blades and a tenon jig on a 10" table saw. Before cutting the stock, score along a line marked 3/4" (19 mm) from the ends of the side rails with an oscillating tool (or a dove-tail saw). Pre-cutting the line helps prevent tear-out on each end. It also a good idea to have a set of sharp dado blades.

Set up the side rails on top of the transverse rails. Mark their positions according to the desired dimensions for each seat (refer to the table on the previous page). Mark the position of each mortise on the transverse rails.

(Bottom left) Use a pencil to mark the positions of the side rail tenons on the transverse rails.

(Bottom right) Use a marking gauge to mark the position of the 3/8" (9 mm) mortises on the transverse rails.

Excavate the mortises on the transverse rails with a 3/8" mortise chisel and a wooden mallet. The excavation process starts by making a vertical cut at each end of the mortise.

Next, make a series of angled cuts along the full length of the mortise between the end-cuts. Then, remove the wood chips to excavate about 1/8" (3 mm) deep. After about 6 repetitions, the mortise is excavated to the desired ¾" (19mm) depth.

The tenons fit into the mortises to create the frame. The original seat frame joints were not glued. They were held together with the tension of the cane. You can stabilize the joints with some waterproof glue, if you wish. However, it is not really necessary and the original builders did not use gluev in the joints. The frames are then sanded lightly. I usually progress in steps to 220-grit sandpaper.

(Top left) The ends of the mortise are cut with a mortise chisel held vertically.

(Top right) A mortise chisel is held at an angle and cuts small pieces the length of the mortise.

(Middle left) Each pass with the mortising chisel cuts another 1/8" (3 mm) deeper into the transverse rail.

(Middle right) The completed mortise is at least 3/4" (19 mm) deep.

(Bottom) The mortise and tenon joints in seat frames are made with a wooden mallet, a mortising chisel and a marking gauge.

Mark the layout lines for the positions of the holes on each frame. This starts with edge lines set ½" (13 mm) from the inside edges of each frame. Then, mark the position of each hole. The transverse rails of the bow seat have 17 holes (including the corners) while the stern seat rails have 13 holes. They are spaced approximately ¾" (19 mm) apart. The side rails of both seats have 7 holes (not including the corners) spaced approximately 1" (25 mm) apart. A tape measure helps position the holes, but don't worry about precision. The holes in the original seat frames were positioned by eye. In fact, you can recognize an original seat frame by the uneven spacing between the holes.

Before drilling the hole, take a few minutes with a steel punch to make a small dent at each hole position. The dents help capture the bit and prevent it from wandering. Another option is to use a brad point drill bit.

The holes are 3/16" (5 mm) in diameter. Once drilled, give the frames a final light sanding to clean up wood fragments around the holes and to remove the pencil lines.

Originally, the seat frames were caned prior to the application of any finish. However, as with everything else in the canoe, it is a good idea to protect the wood first. Once the frames are stained, shellacked and varnished, you are ready to start weaving the cane.

(Top left) Use a marking guage to mark 1/2" (13 mm) from the inside edges of the seat frame. Extend a pencil line the full length of each side.

(Top right) A pencil marks the position of each hole in the seat frame for hand-woven cane.

(Bottom) Holes are drilled with a 3/16" (5 mm) bit.

Cane "Rattan" Seats

Whether you are working with original seats or making replicas, once the frames are refinished, they need to be woven in the original pattern.

It is called a "quick" pattern because it involves a six-stage pattern in which only the two diagonal stages are woven. The two vertical strands are established first followed by the two horizontal strand which lay directly on top of the vertical strands. No weaving is involved to this point. Then, both diagonals are woven in the same manner – under the vertical strands and over the horizontals.

Calling the pattern quick is relative, I suppose. Having done several dozen seats, it takes me four to six hours to do each seat as opposed to the eight to ten hours my first time. I do this work in the evening while watching a movie (or three). Select about 20 lengths of natural strand cane (most canoe seats use 3 mm cane also called medium cane) and soak them in warm water for 10 to 15 minutes.

Wrap the strands in a moist towel and sit down with a pair of scissors (I use Chinese gardening shears), a caning stiletto and about six hardwood pegs (I use golf tees as well as some pegs I whittled from hardwood scraps).

(Top right) The first stage of the caning pattern sets down vertical strands from one transverse rail to the other. The strands are snug but not tight.

(Bottom right) Strand ends are tied off at the back of the seat with a half-hitch.

(Below) Caning equipment includes hardwood pegs, a pair of shears and a caning awl (stiletto).

The first stage of the pattern consists of a series of parallel strands running from one transverse rail to the other. I call these the vertical strands. Start by inserting the strand from the topside of the frame into the hole on the transverse rail just left of the corner hole. Feed the strand through to the underside of the frame until about 4" (10 cm) of cane extends through. It will be tied off when this stage is completed. Hold it in place with a wooden peg inserted on the topside of the frame. Pull the strand across the frame to the other transverse rail. Insert the strand into the hole just left of the corner hole. Feed the entire strand through the hole from the topside to the underside. Make sure the cane sits flat and untwisted with the shiny side up. Pull the cane firmly but not overly tight and hold it in place with another peg. Feed the free-end of the strand into the next hole in the row on the transverse rail, pull it up through the hole to the topside, hold it in place with another peg (shiny side up) and start again.

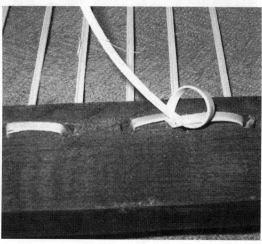

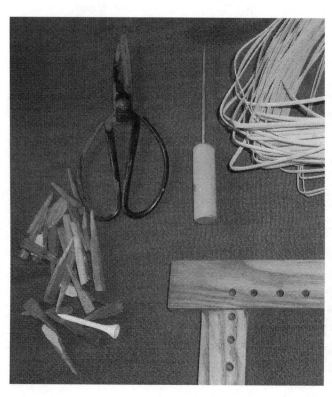

When you come to the end of a strand, tie it off with a simple half-hitch knot on the underside of the frame. Keep the strand moist as you work. A dry strand will break when you tie it tight on the underside of the frame.

(Top) The second stage sits adjacent to the first stage.

The second stage of the pattern is another set of vertical strands. Pull the first strand to one side as the second strand is brought down next to it. Everything will work out as you weave later strands. Just make sure that the second strand does not lie directly on top of the first strand. Once finished and allowed to dry, the cane will tighten on its own.

(Middle) The third stage runs from one side of the seat to the other and lies directly on top of the first and second stages -- no weaving.

The third stage runs from one side rail on the frame to the other. I call these the horizontal strands. The third strand is woven in the same manner as the first vertical strand.

(Bottom) The fourth stage sits adjacent to the third stage.

The fourth stage is the same as the second stage. Again, ensure that the strands are sitting side-by-side.

Because none of the stands so far have been woven, any twists in the cane can be straightened as each strand is drawn tight. However, from here on, make sure each strand is straight before you begin to weave it into the pattern. If a twist occurs, pull the strand out and begin again.

(Top left) The fifth stage starts in the top right-hand corner of the seat frame. Weave the cane under the vertical strands and over the horizontal strands.

(Top right) After weaving the strand under the last set of vertical strands, pull it through the hole to the left of the last vertical strands.

The fifth stage begins in the top-right corner of the frame. Feed one end of the strand through the corner hole from the topside and leave about 4" (10 cm) extending through on the underside. Tie off this end on the underside. Hold the strand in place by inserting a peg into the corner hole from the topside. Trim the free end by cutting on a diagonal to create a point. This pointed end is easier to weave.

The weaving pattern is always the same – under the vertical strands and over the horizontals. Beginning at the first set of vertical strands to the left of the corner hole, weave the free end of the strand under the first set of vertical strands and over the first set of horizontal strands. Move left to the next vertical strands and continue weaving until you complete three or four sets of vertical and horizontal strands. Then, pull the entire piece of cane through to tighten the strand.

Continue weaving the rest of the strand until you weave under the last set of vertical strands at the bottom of the frame. At this point, pull the piece of cane through again to tighten the entire strand. Make sure that the strand is straight without any twists.

Once in place, insert the cane into the hole immediately left of the last set of vertical strands at the bottom of the frame. Pull the cane through to the underside and use a peg on the topside to hold it in place. The peg is moved over to the next hole once the cane is threaded up through it to the topside.

The weaving proceeds from the current transverse rail to the opposite rail in the same fashion as before. Each new woven strand is made by moving one hole to the left each time.

Eventually, every hole on the transverse rails is woven with cane in the fifth stage. So too, every hole on the sides is woven with cane -

(Bottom left) The fifth stage continues until you reach the bottom left-hand corner.

(Bottom right) Make sure there are two strands in each corner hole.

(Top) The final strand in the bottom right-hand corner (and top left-hand corner) of the fifth stage does not involve any weaving.

except for the corner holes in the top left and bottom right. Since the corner holes in the top right and the bottom left are both transverse and side holes, these two corner holes have two strands woven into them in the fifth stage of the pattern - one for the transverse series and the other of the side series. Therefore, where the first strand in the corner started by going under the vertical strands, the second strand in that hole starts by going over the horizontal strands. Every strand on the side rails starts (and finishes) by going over the horizontal strands. The fifth strand is completed at the opposite corner with a simple, unwoven strand which is then tied off at the back.

The sixth-stage replicates the fifth by weaving under the verticals and over the horizontals. The only difference is that it starts in the top-left corner.

In the sixth stage pattern, corner holes in the top left and bottom right are both transverse and side holes. Therefore, just as in the fifth stage of the pattern, both of these holes receives two strands of cane. The first strand is woven over the last simple strand in the fifth stage. Then the second strand is woven under that same strand. Note that the strands along the sides of the seat frame are woven under the fifth strand.

(Bottom left) The sixth stage starts in the top left-hand corner. It weaves over the last strand in the fifth stage, then under the vertical strands and over the horizontal strands as before.

(Bottom right) At the corners for the sixth stage, the second strand for the corner weaves under the last strand of the fifth stage before entering the corner hole.

81

(Top) A strand of 3mm cane is laid on top of the holes around the perimeter of the woven seat.

Most hand-woven seats are finished with border strands that cover the holes in the frame. These border strands are 3mm wide and are tied into the back of the frame as usual.

The border is held in place with 2.5 mm cane (fine cane). It is tied into the underside of the frame, comes up through the hole, over the border strand and back down through the same hole. This is called couching and is done at every second hole around the border. This is a simple stage in the weaving process but is very time consuming since the stiletto must be used to open each hole enough to allow the couching cane to be threaded through.

(Bottom) The border strand is "couched" by looping 2.5 mm cane up from the back of the seat, over the border strand on one side and then back down through the same hole again. Do this at every second hole arond the seat.

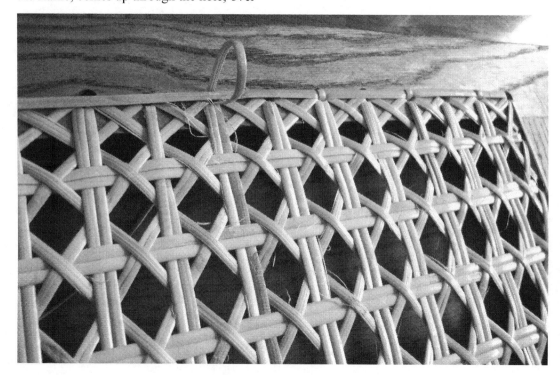

Rawhide "Babiche" Seats

If the seats in your canoe are laced with rawhide similar to that in old snowshoes, chances are you own a "Huron" canoe – the generic name for canoes built in Huron Village (renamed Wendake in 1986). I describe these canoes in detail in Chapter 12. Right now, let's look at these classic Canadian canoe seats. The "babiche" is likely to last longer than the canoe, but at some point you may need to re-lace the seat frames.

The Frame

Seat frames for "Huron" canoes are constructed of birch or maple and assembled with mortise and tenon joints that are very rough and loose. No glue is used, so the rawhide lacing is the only thing holding the frames together.

Refer to the table below for the seat dimensions. As with all of the other components in a canoe, I prefer to apply finish to the frames before I lace them.

Rawhide "Babiche" Seat Frame Dimensions

Component	Position	Imperial	Metric
Transverse rail	Bow	32.00"	81.0 cm
(length)	Stern	20.00"	51.0 cm
Side rail	Bow	8.25"	21.0 cm
(length)	Stern	8.25"	21.0 cm
Horizontal width	Bow	13.25"	33.7 cm
(internal)	Stern	9.75"	24.8 cm
Vertical width	Bow	6.75"	17.1 cm
(internal)	Stern	6.75"	17.1 cm
Seat frame stock	Width	1-3/8"	35.0 mm
	Thickness	7/8"	22.0 mm
Tenon	Width	1-1/8"	29.0 mm
	Height	3/4"	19.0 mm
	Thickness	3/8"	9.5 mm

Rawhide "Babiche" Seat Frame

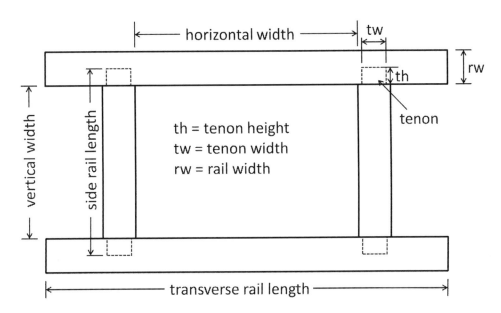

th = tenon height
tw = tenon width
rw = rail width

(Right) Rawhide lace 3/16"
(5 mm) thick is soaked in
water and a little borax for
several hours. Keep it damp as
you work.

The bow seat requires about 65' (20 meters) of 3/16" (5 mm) rawhide lace while the stern seat requires about 50' (15 meters).

The lacing is usually shipped in a long tube and is as hard as a rock. It has to be soaked for several hours before it can be used to lace the seats. I use the bath tub at home and add a little borax to the water to help loosen the rawhide and make it easier to manipulate.

It will take a few hours to lace a seat, so keep a large bowl of water nearby in order to re-soak the lacing as you work.

Handling rawhide lace for several hours can be hard on the hands and the borax can really dry out your skin. Use a hand lotion both before and after lacing a seat to help avoid damage to your skin.

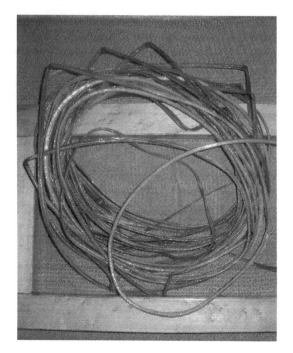

(Below) An eight-stage lacing
pattern creates a "Huron"
stern canoe seat.

Lacing Pattern for a "Huron" Canoe Seat

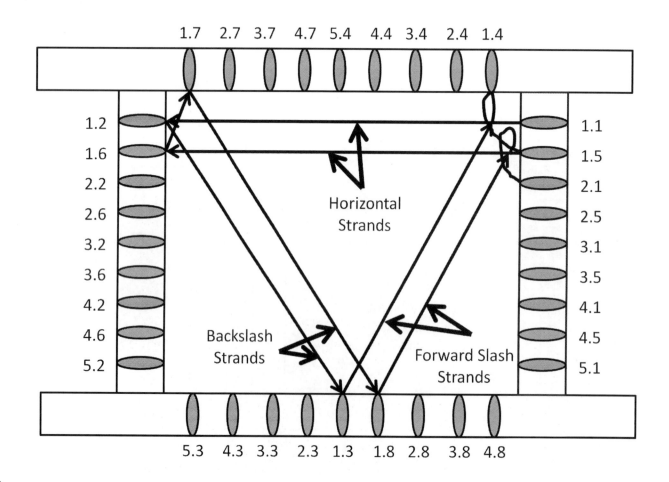

The Pattern

The lacing pattern I describe is the most common one found in canoe seats. It is by no means the only one. The process can be applied to all the other patterns. However, some are more complicated than others.

The stern seat has 36 anchor-points – 9 on each of the 4 frame rails. The bow seat is wider than the stern seat. Therefore, it usually has 11 anchor-points on each of the frame rails. In order to make this fit, the anchor-points on the side rails are placed very close together. This will provide enough room for one more complete repetition of the pattern.

Lacing the Seat

The only tool I use is a sharp pocket knife. It trims the lacing and cuts small slits in the ends of pieces for joining. The entire pattern is laced using just a few basic knots and joins. The starting anchor join at 1.1 is made by threading the lace through a small slit in the end of the first lace in the pattern. Throughout the lacing pattern, pull the rawhide firmly but not tight. As the rawhide dries, it becomes very tight.

All of the remaining anchor points are tied using a larks-head knot. To perform this knot, you start by passing the lace over the frame. Wrap around to come up on the "outer" side of the lace and pass over the strand that was just made. Bring the lace back under the frame, then around to finally pass back over the frame and under the lace "bridge" to form the knot. In this case, a picture is worth a thousand words, so use the photo as your guide.

(Top) Cut a slit near the end of the lace and thread the other end through to create a loop for the first anchor point in the pattern.

(Bottom) A larks-head knot is used at all anchor points - except for the first. It is easy to do and difficult to describe, so a picture is worth a thousand words.

(Top) After securing the larkshead knot at 1.4, pass the lace over the horizontal strand and then under the "forward slash" strand. Again, a picture is worth 1,000 words.

Anchor-points 1.2, 1.3 and 1.4 form a triangle pattern on the frame. As you go from 1.3 to create the anchor-point at 1.4, pass the strand under the horizontal. The strand then passes over the horizontal and under the diagonal "forward slash" (/) strand before tying off at anchor point 1.5. All subsequent weaving in the fourth strand follows this pattern.

The fifth strand of the pattern passes over the forward slash strand and under the "backslash" (\ ) strand before tying off at anchor point 1.6. All of the subsequent weaving in the fifth strand follows this pattern.

The sixth strand weaves over the "backslash" strand and under the horizontal strand before tying off at anchor point 1.7. All of the subsequent weaving in the sixth strand follows this pattern.

(Bottom right) The sixth strand passes over the "backslash" and under the horizontal.

(Bottom left) The fifth strand passes over the "forward slash" and under the "backslash".

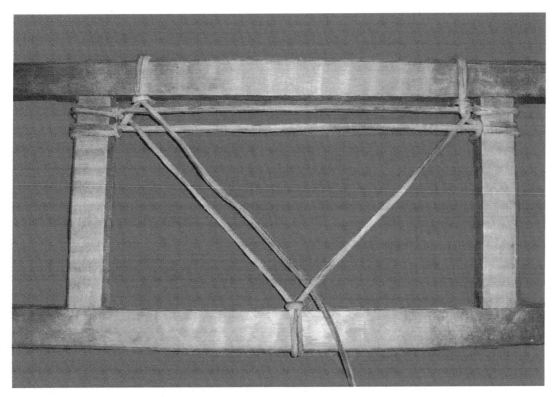

The seventh strand passes over the horizontal strands and under the "forward slash" strand before tying off at anchor point 1.8. All subsequent weaving in the seventh strand follows this pattern.

The eighth strand does not have any weaving, but it finishes by passing over both the fourth and the fifth strands at the fifth anchor-point in that repetition of the pattern. It wraps under the strands and then up and over itself before forming the first anchor-point in the next repetition of the pattern.

From now on the pattern is repeated with one addition. After forming the second anchor-point in the pattern and before weaving the second strand, stabilize it by passing over both the fifth and seventh strands of the previous set, then come up and over itself. The second strand requires no weaving.

The seat is woven with progressively more and more weaving required as each set of the pattern is performed.

(Bottom left) After forming the eighth strand, anchor it around the fourth and fifth strands. Then, tie a larks-head knot at position 2.1.

(Bottom right) The tenth strand is anchored around the fifth and sixth strands before forming the next "backslash".

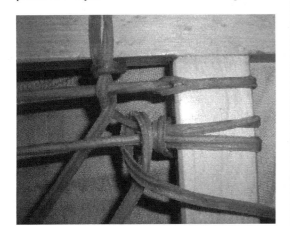

(Top) Progressively more weaving is required as each repetition of the pattern is completed.

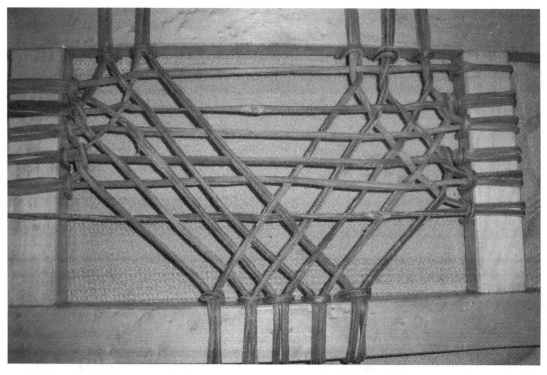

(Bottom right) Once the seat lacing is completed, tie off the last anchor point with a half-hitch or two.

(Bottom left) Cut a slit in the end of both the current piece of lace and the piece you want as the extension. Slip the current end through the hole in the extension. Then, thread the extension lace through the hole in the current lace.

At some point, usually two or three times in a given seat, you come to the end of a piece of rawhide lace. To continue weaving, join the next lace to the previous one. The joins are made by cutting a small slit in each end. The end of the old strand is passed through the slit in the new strand. The entire new strand is then fed through the slit in the end of the old strand to create a secure join. I like to locate the joins so they lie on the underside of the frame.

Once you have completed the lacing pattern, the last larks-head knot is tied at the final anchor-point and the rawhide is knotted with one or two half-hitches.

Allow the rawhide to dry for a couple of days. Then apply a mixture of two parts boiled linseed oil and one part turpentine. Let the oil mixture dry for at least a week.

The seat will be finished with shellac and varnished along with the rest of the new wood in the canoe. This process is described in Chapter 9.

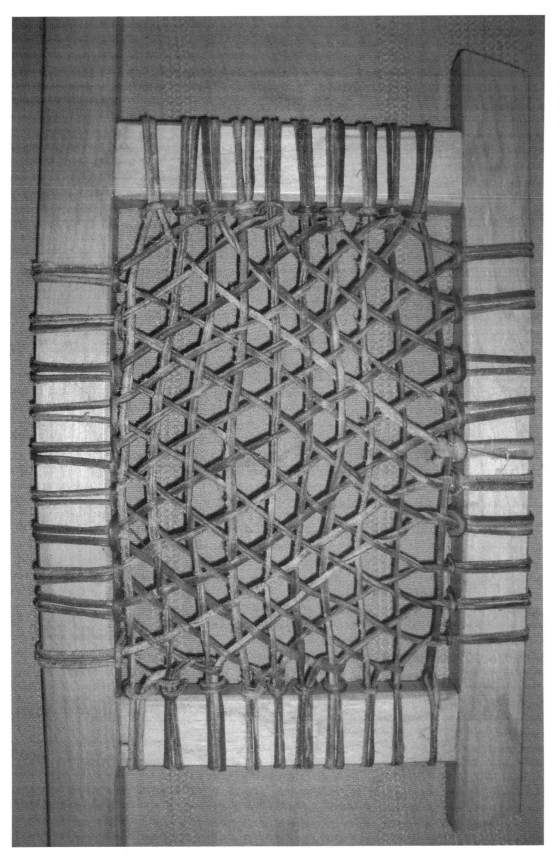

The lacing in a new "Huron" canoe seat is complete. Apply a mixture of two parts double boiled linseed oil and one part turpentine to the rawhide after it has dried overnight. Allow the oil mixture to dry for at least a week before applying shellac and varnish.

(Right) A regular canoe thwart will press against the bone at the base of the neck while you carry your canoe from one place to another. Portaging is literally a pain in the neck.

Thwarts/Portage Yoke

When someone asks me to restore their canoe, they usually want it to look just as it did when it came out of the factory 40 or 50 years ago. However, one change they often ask for is a portage yoke patterned after those made by Chestnut to replace the centre thwart.

Northern Canada is a landscape consisting of more water than land. One of the unique features of Canadian canoes is the fact that they have legs. People simply pick up their canoe and carry it from one lake or river to another. The task of carrying the canoe is made more comfortable by replacing the centre thwart with a carrying yoke. One of the carrying yokes produced by the Chestnut Canoe Company is a perfect example of form and function combining to create a design that is beautiful in its simplicity. One curious feature of this design is a "little notch" carved in the centre of the yoke.

The Chestnut yoke design accommodates the spinous process of the seventh cervical vertebra (C7) at the base of the neck. Please excuse the anatomical jargon, but you all know what I'm referring to. You become acutely aware of it every time you throw a canoe up onto your shoulders. The centre thwart digs into your neck resulting in significant discomfort. It is quite literally a pain in the neck. The Chestnut notch alleviates the pressure and makes the portage much more comfortable.

(Below) Use a saber saw (or band saw) to cut the blank shape of the yoke.

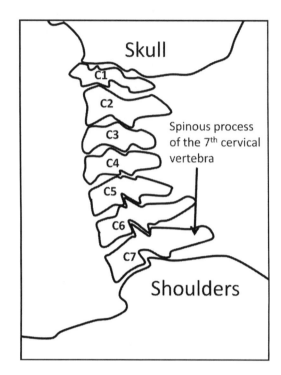

Skull
C1
C2
C3
C4
Spinous process of the 7th cervical vertebra
C5
C6
C7
Shoulders

To make a Chestnut carrying yoke, I first make a template. You can use cardboard, but I prefer ¼" panel board to make something I can use repeatedly over the years. The plan I present on page 92 is taken directly from an original Chestnut yoke. Use a permanent ink marker to transfer the shape onto a piece of hardwood 1" (25 mm) thick. Cut the basic shape with a band saw or saber saw. The curve in the centre of the yoke is best cut by removing the wood in a series of small sections.

Carving the final shape of the yoke can be done in a number of ways. Some people use a large gouge and a mallet. I use an angle grinder set up with a 24-grit sanding disc. With this, I do the bulk of the carving in about 15 minutes. The hardwood can be dished out to about ½" (13 mm) thick in the centre of the yoke. I use a pair of outside calipers to check the thickness as I go. You can also check the yoke for fit from time to time by pressing the yoke onto your shoulders. I know I've got the notch the right size when I no longer feel any pressure on C7. Finally, carve the ends of the yoke down to a thickness of ¾" (19 mm) to match the thickness of the original thwart.

The yoke is sanded smooth with a random-orbital sander in progressions from 60-grit to 220-grit. As with every component of the canoe that gets handled a lot, moisten the wood to raise the grain and then polish the hardwood yoke by hand in progressions from 320-grit to 600-grit.

Stain your new yoke to match the original wood. As with the rest of the new wood in your canoe, the yoke will be finished with shellac and varnish as described in Chapter 9.

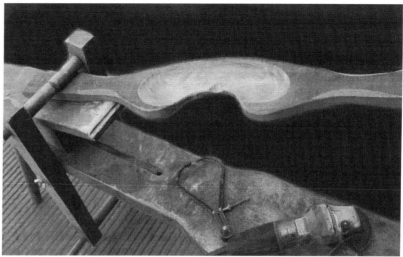

(Top right) Check the thickness of the dish in the yoke with a pair of outside calipers. An angle grinder set up with a 24-grit sanding disc does a great job on the rough carving.

(Top left) Use a random-orbital sander to work from 60-grit to 220-grit sandpaper. Wet the wood to raise the grain. Then, polish the yoke to 600-grit.

(Left) Stain the new wood to match the original wood in the canoe.

(Bottom) This new portage yoke is made from solid cherry. When finished, all you want to do is touch it.

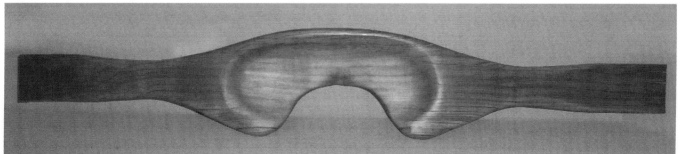

*The plan for a Chestnut Canoe
Company Portage Yoke.*

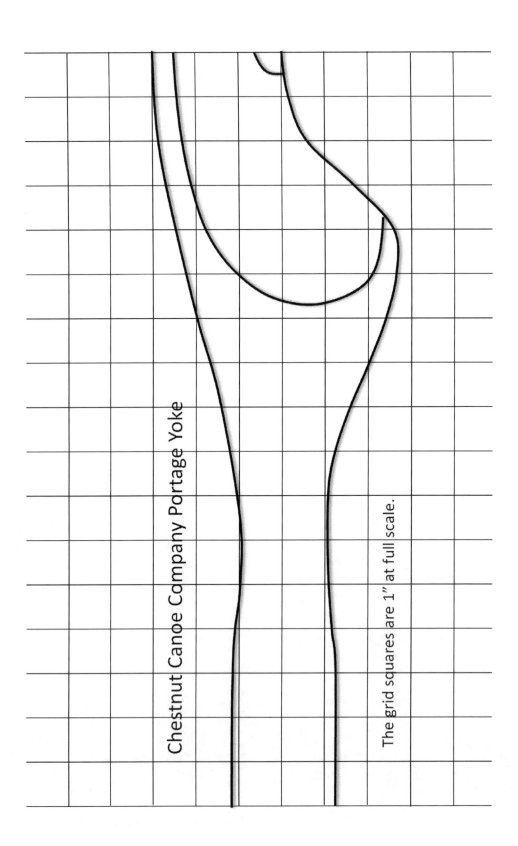

Chestnut Canoe Company Portage Yoke

The grid squares are 1" at full scale.

7
Canvas

For many people, all of the work to this point amounts to nothing more than a very challenging woodwork project. It is not really a canoe restoration until a new canvas is stretched onto the hull. Months of hard work and frustrations as well as the many successes and triumphs seem to fade into memory as the "skin" goes on. I can feel you taking a deep breath to brace yourself for what many see as the most difficult part of the project. I invite you to relax a little and learn a process that is little more than an upholstery job. This procedure is not without its pitfalls, but it's far from the scary menace that some would have you believe. So, let's get into the magic of re-canvassing your canoe. For those of you with a vee-stern canoe, the process of stretching a new canvas onto one of these will be discussed separately. Following that, we will explore one of the great "trade secrets" in the world of canvas-covered canoes – canvas filler. This chapter concludes with a discussion about a few synthetic materials that may be considered, by some, as alternatives to canvas.

Preparations

Before stretching the canvas, spend a few hours checking every tack in the canoe. Re-clinch any tacks that are not flush with the hull. Replace loose tacks with new ones in undamaged wood. Apply wood filler to any small holes or gouges in the exterior of the hull. These are usually a result of removing old tacks. Stain all of the new wood to match the original wood. To determine the colour of the original wood, wipe a small section with lacquer thinner. The wet wood shows the final colour and dries quickly. Allow both the stain and wood filler to dry overnight.

The next day, sand the hull exterior lightly with 80-grit sandpaper. Brush away any dust and debris on the hull, and apply a mixture of two parts double boiled linseed oil and one part turpentine. If you stripped the old varnish out of the interior, then oil the entire canoe. Otherwise, apply the oil mixture to the hull exterior and use a rag to wipe up any oil that dripped into the interior. Some very old, dry canoes require several of coats of oil over a period of many days. Allow the oil to dry for a week or two at room temperature.

Canvas Stretching Setup

Half the battle in the canvas job is setting up for the task. There are as many techniques as there are canoe restorers. Some people stretch the canvas with the canoe held upside-down on sawhorses. At wooden canoe festivals, they often get a dozen people together to stretch the canvas by hand.

I use a method that is close to what was done in the original canoe factories: setting the canoe into the canvas envelope right-side-up. So, here is my setup.

The canvas envelope is secured at both ends with a clamping system described later in this chapter. One end is attached directly to a wall or solid beam. The stretching process involves a great deal of tension, so make sure that your anchor-points are very strong and solid. The other end of the canvas is attached to a come-along that is attached to another solid wall or beam. The position of the canvas clamping system at this end is adjust-able according to the length of the canoe being canvassed. The clamping system is suspended from the ceiling. If you are doing only one canoe, the attachment can be an eye bolt secured directly to the ceiling. I have an adjustable system comprised of a length of 1" (25 mm) steel pipe suspended horizontally about 8" (20 cm) from the ceiling by a couple of hardwood blocks. A carabiner is hooked onto the steel pipe and slides along its full length. A length of 3/8" (9 mm) rope is attached to the carabiner and the canvas clamping system. This arrangement accommodates canoes that range in length from 12' (3.7 meters) to 18' (5.5 meters). The ends of the canvas envelope are held close to the canoe by means of large hardwood "clothespins" that will be described later in this chapter. The canoe would pop out of the canvas envelope without two vertical struts (spruce 2x4s) to keep the canoe in place. Lengths of spruce 2x6 protect the bottom of the canoe from the pressure exerted by the vertical struts.

Canvas Stretching Setup
Legend

Item	Description
a	Distance from the floor to the anchor-point on a solid beam attached with a carabiner to the come-along – 59" (150 cm)
b	Distance from the floor to the anchor-point on a solid beam attached with a carabiner to the canvas clamping system – 69" (175 cm)
c	Come-along
d	Canvas clamping system
e	Rope used to suspend the canvas clamping system – 3/8" (9 mm) diameter
f	Carabiner slides along the length of a steel pipe
g	Steel pipe – 1" (25 mm) diameter
h	Hardwood block used to suspend the steel pipe from the ceiling
i	Hardwood "clothespin" used to close the canvas envelope at the ends of the canoe
j	Spruce 2x4 strut used to push the canoe into the canvas envelope
k	Spruce 2x6 boards used to protect the bottom of the canoe
l	Canvas envelope
m	Canoe sitting inside the canvas envelope

Canvas Stretching Setup

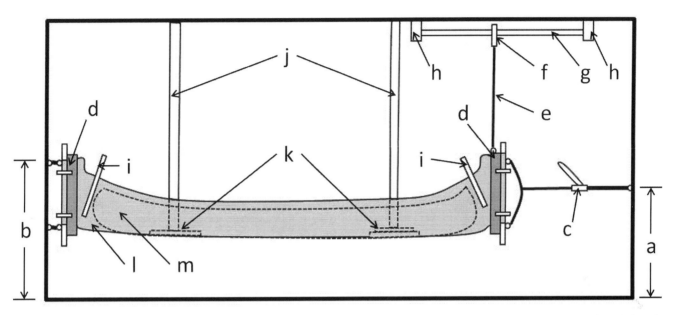

(Above) Refer to the legend on page 90 for a description of the component parts of the canvas stretching setup.

Canvas Clamping System

My system for securing the canvas at both ends of the envelope is patterned after that described by Wally Hodge in the December 1996 issue of *Wooden Canoe* magazine (refer to illustrations on page 96). The system consists of two 2x4's 42" (107 cm) long. Wally recommended hardwood but I find that regular spruce 2x4's work just fine. Each has two 3/8" (9 mm) eye bolts drilled through the width of the 2x4 near each end. They are backed by washers to ensure a strong fit.

The end of the canvas envelope is folded around a 1" (25 mm) dowel rod that is about 48" (120 cm) long. Place one of the 2x4's on each side of the canvas fold. The dowel seats snugly into a ¾" (19 mm) cut away corner (called a chamfer) on the inside-back edge of each 2x4.

The 2x4's are then held together securely with two C-clamps. Heavy rope is fed through the eye bolts and tied into a loop. Carabiners are hooked onto the rope loop to attach the clamping system to both the fixed anchor-point and the come-along.

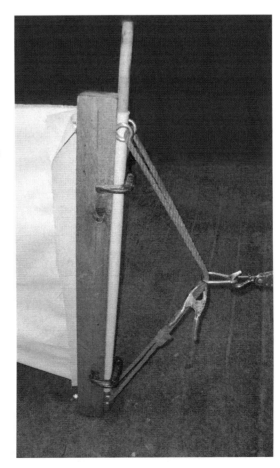

(Right) The canvas clamping system is attached to the come-along with a carabiner.

Canvas Clamping System

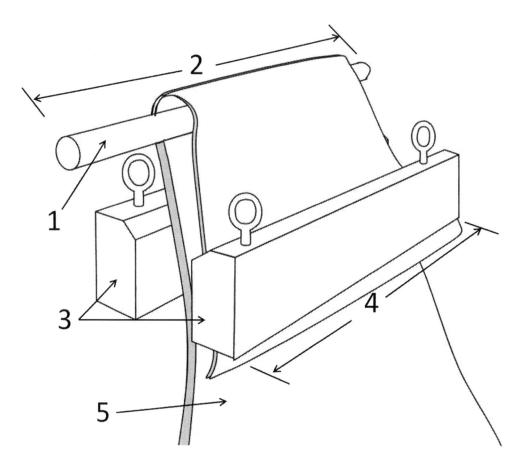

(Below) A cross-section diagram of the canvas clamping system.

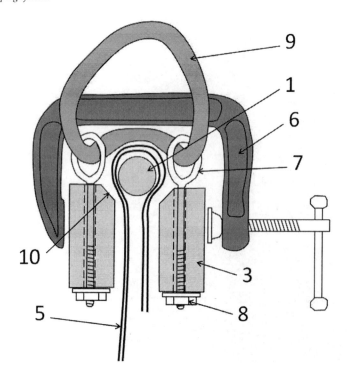

**Canvas Clamping System
Legend**

Item	Description
1	Hardwood dowel – 1" (25 mm) diameter
2	Dowel length – 48" (122 cm)
3	Spruce 2x4
4	2x4 length – 42" (107 cm)
5	Canvas
6	C-clamp
7	Eye bolt – 3/8" (9 mm)
8	Nut and washer – 3/8" (9 mm)
9	Rope – 1/2" (13 mm)
10	3/4" (19 mm) chamfer in the 2x4 to seat the dowel

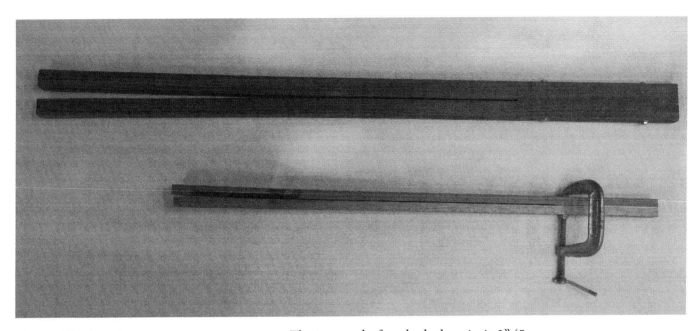

Canvas Clothespin

At the ends of the canoe, the canvas envelope has to be held close to the hull as it is stretched and tacked along the sheer-line. The tool used for this is called a "clothespin" even though it is about ten times larger than any regular clothespin.

They are made of hardwood about 7/8" (22 mm) thick. You will need two clothespins, so cut two pieces about 35" (90 cm) long and 2" (5 cm) wide. Make another cut on the table saw to slice each 2" piece down the middle leaving about 8" (20 cm) uncut at one end.

The top-end of each clothespin is 2" (5 cm) wide. If you use them like this, the wood is likely to split under the pressure exerted by the canvas envelope. Therefore, the top-end of each clothespin needs to be stabilized. This can be done with a couple of 10-24 carriage bolts. When I did my first canoe, I stabilized the top-end of each clothespin with a C-clamp as a quick and easy way of making what I thought was going to be a temporary tool. I ended up using my temporary, makeshift clothespins for about 20 years. They did the job for about 200 canoes.

(Above) The canvas "clothes-pins" can be made to last and stabilized at the top-end with a couple of bolts (top) or thrown together in a makeshift manner and stabilized at the top-end with a small C-clamp (bottom).

(Left) The canvas "clothespins" close the canvas envelope at each end of the canoe.

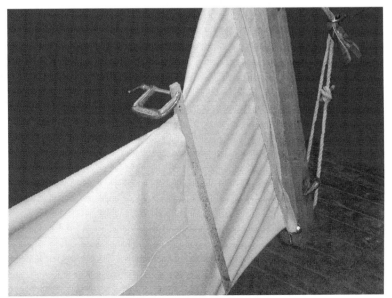

(Top left) Turn the canoe upside-down in the cradles and drape the canvas over the hull. Leave at least 3' (90 cm) of canvas extending past both ends of the canoe. Secure the canvas to the canoe with two spring clamps on each side at the sheer-line.

(Top right) Turn the canoe right-side up in the cradles with the canvas draped around the outside of the hull.

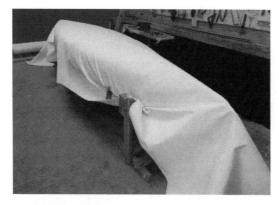

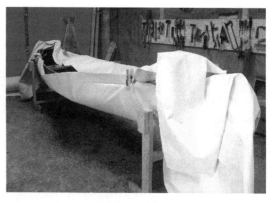

Assembling the Stretching System

Start by checking the hull one last time. Brush the hull again to make sure there is nothing clinging. When the canvas is stretched tight, even a small bit of sawdust will show up as a bump.

Now, let's talk about canvas. I normally use #10 untreated artist canvas weighing 14.5 ounces per square yard. Canvas 72" wide will work for most canoes. Large canoes, such as freighters, often require canvas that is 96" wide. Since I purchase canvas in 100 meter rolls, I have the advantage of being able to set up the roll on a rack.

To set up the stretching system, turn the canoe upside-down in the cradles. Drape the canvas over the bottom of the hull. Make

sure there is at least 18" (45 cm) of canvas extending past each end of the canoe.

Secure the canvas to the inwales with two spring clamps on either side of the canoe. Turn the canoe rightside-up. Attach a canvas clamping system to each end of the canvas. This forms an envelope with the canoe sitting inside. Secure one canvas clamp system to the fixed anchor-point in a solid wall or beam. Then, secure the other canvas clamp system to the come-along. Suspend that canvas clamp system from the ceiling by means of a length of 3/8" (9 mm) rope. Make sure that both canvas clamp systems are at approximately the same height. With everything in place, remove the cradles and make sure the canoe is sitting squarely in the centre of the canvas envelope.

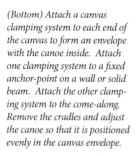

(Bottom) Attach a canvas clamping system to each end of the canvas to form an envelope with the canoe inside. Attach one clamping system to a fixed anchor-point on a wall or solid beam. Attach the other clamping system to the come-along. Remove the cradles and adjust the canoe so that it is positioned evenly in the canvas envelope.

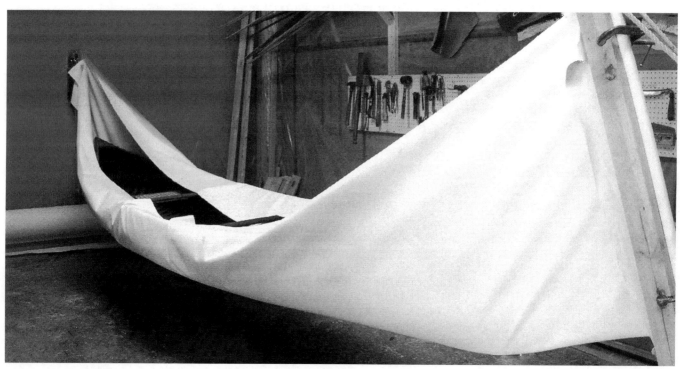

Wedge two vertical struts (I use 2x4s) between the ceiling and the canoe. My shop is an old warehouse with thick fir planks in the ceiling. Other locations would require re-enforcements in the ceiling Set the bottom end of each vertical strut on a 2' (60 cm) length of 2x6 to protect the bottom of the canoe. Position the bottom end of each vertical strut further away from the come-along than the top end. As tension is applied, the bottom end of each strut is pulled closer to the come-along and brings the struts closer to plumb. Another option is to weigh down the canoe. I've used a number of 5-gallon pails filled with sand to push the canoe into the envelope as the canvas is stretched lengthwise. Crank the come-along a number of times to take up the slack. ***Make sure that all of the clamps and struts are secure.***

At a position on the top edge of the canvas envelope that is in-line vertically with the end of the canoe, cut straight down the canvas stopping about 4" (10 cm) from the sheer-line of the canoe.

Hold the canvas close to ends of the canoe with the "clothespins".

Trim the canvas along the sheer-line on both sides of the canoe to leave about 3" (8 cm) of canvas extending above the top of the inwales. Leave enough canvas above the canoe to provide a good grip for the canvas pliers that will be used to stretch the canvas at the sheer-line.

Trim the canvas with a utility knife and a new, sharp blade. ***Don't cut too close to the top of the inwales.*** Start by trimming down to about 6" (15 cm) above the top of the inwales. Trim more as required when you start using the canvas pliers to stretch the canvas. Once you have canvassed several dozen canoes, you will be able to trim the canvas to the desired height with one practised cut. Until then, however, take your time and trim down in small increments.

(Left) Set the vertical struts in place to press the canoe into the canvas envelope.

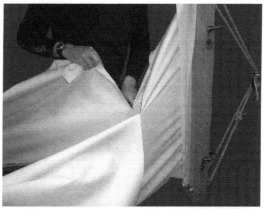

(Left) Cut straight down from the top-edge of the canvas envelope at a point vertically in-line with each end of the canoe. Stop the cut about 4" (10 cm) above the top of the stem-end.

(Left) Set the "clothespin" to hold the canvas envelope close to the canoe at each end.

*(Left) Trim the canvas about 3" (8 cm) above the top of the inwales. **Do not cut too close to the inwales.***

(Right) Grab the canvas with canvas pliers. Hook the fulcrum of the pliers over the inside edge of the inwale. Rock the pliers back to stretch the canvas. Drive a tack at the top edge of the planking over the rib top.

Stretching Canvas

Once the canvas is trimmed all the way around the canoe, the come-along is cranked until the canvas is stretched tightly around the canoe. The amount of tension required varies with each canoe. Tap the canvas at the end closest to the come-along. When it rings like a tenor drum, grab your canvas pliers and cobbler's hammer and start to attach the canvas along the sides.

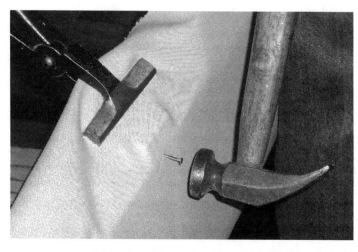

Starting at the centre of the canoe, pull the canvas tight with canvas pliers. To do this, rest the jaws of the pliers on the top of the inwale and grab the canvas. With the canvas held firmly, draw the pliers toward the centre-line of the canoe and hook the large "fulcrum" of the pliers over the inside corner of the inwale. Rock the pliers to about a 45° angle and secure the canvas at the top of the planking with a 7/8" (22 mm) brass tack.

Secure the canvas at four rib-tops on both sides of the canoe near the centre. If you see loose, sagging canvas between the tacks, more lengthwise tension is required. If so, re-move three of the four tacks on one side and crank the come-along a number of "clicks". Re-tack the canvas and check to see if the sags are gone. If not, repeat the process with more "clicks" in the come-along.

There is a "feel" developed in terms of the amount of tension needed to achieve a smooth fit. The shape of the hull in your canoe will affect the amount of tension required. Gener-ally speaking, hulls with more tumblehome re-quire more lengthwise tension but there is no set formula. If it is your first time, just keep an eye on the sags between the tacks. When they disappear (or close to it), the tension is right. Small sags between the tacks will dis-appear when filler is applied to the canvas, so there is some leeway in the process.

Once proper tension is achieved, attach the canvas at three or four more rib-tops on both sides of the canoe. Work from the centre towards both ends. As with most things described in this book, your first attempts in-volve a lot of trial-and-error (with an emphasis on error). It is all part of the learning process.

(Bottom) Start stretching the canvas at the centre of the canoe. Drive four tacks into four rib tops on both sides of the canoe. If there are noticeable sags in the canvas between the tacks, remove the tacks. Increase the tension in the come-along and repeat the process until the canvas is smooth between the tacks.

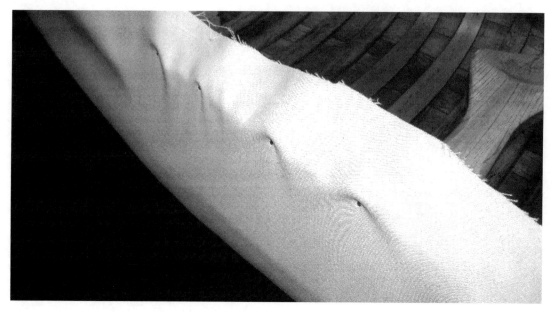

Having attached the canvas to every rib-top, release the tension from the come-along and remove the struts. Support the canoe with the cradles and cut the canvas away from the clamps being sure to leave at least 6" (15 cm) extending past each end of the canoe.

To close the ends of the canvas around each stem, turn the canoe upside-down and raise one end to a comfortable working height. This is done by supporting it on top of the cradle with a scrap length of 2x4. Crease the canvas at the centre-line and cut along the crease from the point where the stem turns away from the canvas at the bottom of the canoe. This creates two flaps of canvas – one on each side. Each flap is trimmed to leave about 3" (8 cm) of canvas extending past the stem profile. Again, care must be taken to avoid cutting the canvas too close. There must be enough material to grab with the canvas pliers.

The end of the canvas is closed around the stem by stretching and tacking one flap around the stem, trimming away the excess canvas and then doing the same on the other side. Start by stretching the canvas at the point where the stem turns up from the bottom. Lever the pliers along the stem and pull the canvas tight along the centre-line of the canoe. Secure the canvas to the stem with 3 or 4 tacks spaced about 1" (2.5 cm) apart. I use short tacks to attach the ends of the canvas to the canoe stem (about 5/8" or 16mm). Next, move to the stem-top and use the pliers to stretch the canvas flap. Make sure the canvas along the sheer line is sag-free, and secure it along the stem with 3 or 4 tacks spaced about 1" (25 mm) apart. I alternate

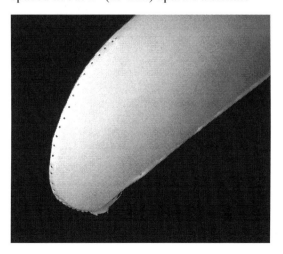

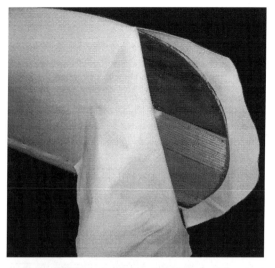

(Top right) Slice the canvas down the centre-line starting at the point where the stem turns away from the bottom of the canoe. Trim the canvas leaving enough for the canvas pliers to grab well.

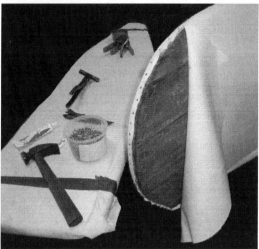

(Bottom right) One side of the canvas is tacked along the stem. An old ironing board makes a convenient, portable table to keep tools within easy reach.

from top to bottom working towards the middle of the stem until the entire flap is tight and securely fastened. Now, trim any excess canvas along the open side of the canoe stem.

The second flap is stretched, tacked and trimmed the same way as the first. As each flap is secured to the stem, check to ensure the canvas is stretched smooth with no sags, creases or puckers. You may have to fuss a bit with the tension of the canvas along the sheer line near the end of the canoe in order to create a tight fit at the bottom of the stem. The length of the cut along the centerline of the canvas may also have to be extended ever so slightly to remove any puckers. All this varies with the shape of the stem profile. Your canoe may be straight-forward or may require some fussing. As long as you stretch the canvas well both where the stem curves away from the bottom and at the stem-top, you ought to avoid any major difficulties.

(Left) Both sides of the canvas are tacked along the stem to close the canvas at the end.

101

Once both ends are closed, support the canoe upside-down on top of the both cradles. Get out the propane torch and remove the nap.

Nap is the fuzzy balls of cotton extending above the weave. It needs to be removed by burning it off with the propane torch. To avoid burning the canvas, keep the torch moving. Start at one end at the top of the stem and move down to the sheer-line. Move over about 4" (10 cm) and pass the torch over the canvas from the sheer-line to the centre-line of the canoe. The path of the torch continues in this manner, moving along the canvas in 4" (10 cm) vertical passes.

Keep an eye open for any thread-ends that may ignite as you pass close to the edges of the canvas. Make sure these are extinguished. Otherwise, the thread will continue to burn like a wick along its full length and cut the canvas in two. I saw this happen once. Fortunately, I was able to extinguish the burning thread before it did irreparable damage.

So, there it is. The canvas is now ready to be filled. You will find the learning curve a little steep. Just remember to breathe and smile. Are we having fun yet?

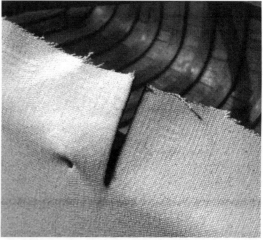

Wood-Canvas Prospector Vee-Stern Canoes

Elk, Bear, Fawn, Marsh, Birch (shown)

Canvassing a Vee-Stern Canoe

Many of the working canoes built in Canada by companies such as the Chestnut Canoe Company had a stern specifically designed to accommodate a small outboard motor. This "vee-stern" is most often found in Chestnut Prospector, Ogilvy and Freighter canoes.

Canvassing a vee-stern starts by setting up your canoe with the bow at the fixed anchor-point end of the canvas envelope. Extend the canvas a total of about 5' (150 cm) past the stern transom. Set up canvas clamping systems at both ends as usual to leave about 4' (120 cm) of canvas between the transom and the canvas clamping system. Place the canvas "clothespin" close to the canvas clamping system at the stern. This allows the canvas to taper smoothly past the transom.

Once the canvas has been stretched and tacked at all of the rib-tops, the canvas is stretched and attached at the transom before the canoe is cut out of the envelope. This is done with a series of long, narrow flaps of canvas cut from the envelope at the stern.

Cut a flap of canvas about 4" (10 cm) wide from the clothespin to about 3" (7.5 cm) from the transom. Do this on both sides. You will eventually have two flaps of canvas on each side of the transom (refer to the pictures on the next page). These flaps are stapled into place on the transom about 1" (25 mm) in from the edge. This process involves a lot of temporary tacks and/or staples, re-stretching and re-attaching both on the transom and along the sheer-line near the transom. Stretch the canvas flaps with canvas pliers

(Top) Vee-stern canoes were designed to take a small outboard motor. (Photo from Chestnut Canoe Company catalogue 1972.)

(Bottom left) The canvas tapers smoothly past the vee-stern when there is about 4' (120 cm) of canvas between the canoe's transom and the canvas "clothespin" (distance A in the photo).

(Bottom right) Cut a flap of canvas about 4" (10 cm) wide on both sides of the transom. Cut to within about 3" (8 cm) of the transom.

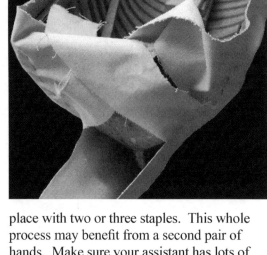

(Top left) Stretch the flaps of canvas tight around the edge of the transom and secure them with staples.

(Top right) When the canvas is stapled for about 8" (20 cm) on both sides of the transom and the canvas along the hull is smooth on both sides of the canoe, cut the canoe from the envelope.

as well as by hand. It is a little fussy and perhaps a little annoying, but you will end up with canvas stretched around the top 8" (20 cm) or so of the transom. This is all done before the canvas is cut out of the envelope.

Create flaps of canvas long enough to reach across the transom and still provide enough cloth to be grabbed by the canvas pliers. Refer to the pictures to get an idea of the end-result. You will be attaching and reattaching the canvas several times on each side of the transom until all of the sags and wrinkles have been removed. It is something that you will figure out as you go along.

Starting at the top of the transom on one side, stretch the canvas flap across to the other side. Use the edge of the transom as a lever-point for the canvas pliers. Remove as many sags and wrinkles as possible. Hold the flap in

place with two or three staples. This whole process may benefit from a second pair of hands. Make sure your assistant has lots of patience and understands that a certain amount of frustration will arise during this process.

Remove a few tacks from the sheer-line on the side of the canoe at the stern. Re-stretch and re-tack the canvas to smooth things out a little. This is a gradual process, so don't expect everything to be smooth the first time around. I use 1/2" (13 mm) staples to attach the canvas to the transom. When staples must be removed, I use a pair of concave cutters.

Once the top section of the canvas flaps have been attached on both sides of the tramsom, cut the second flap on each side. This creates enough slack in the first flap to allow it to be attached completely. Continue until both flap are attached on both sides of the transom.

(Bottom left) Stretch and tack one canvas flap over the stern stem and trim the excess canvas.

(Bottom right) Stretch and tack the second canvas flap over the stern stem, and trim the excess canvas to complete the closure of the stern.

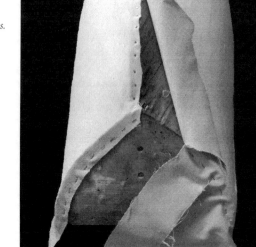

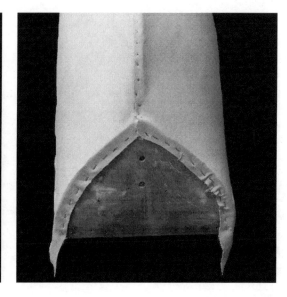

Cut the canoe from the canvas envelope and set it in the cradles as usual. Turn the canoe upside-down and close the stern end as discussed earlier in the chapter. There will be a little fussing as you pull the canvas tight at the point where the transom meets the stem. Do this by hand and remember to stay calm. The canvas edges on the transom are covered with a piece of 3/8" marine plywood. It is sealed with marine bedding compound in the same manner as the keel.

Normally this "transom plate" is removed at the start of the restoration and set aside until it is re-installed. If this is the case, remove old bedding compound and paint with a random-orbital sander and 60-grit sandpaper. Sometimes, when the bedding compound is very thick and hard, I remove it with an angle grinder set up with a 24-grit sanding disk. If you choose to use the grinder, be aware that it is very aggressive and could damage the plywood if you are not careful. I usually use the grinder to remove the bulk of the bedding compound and finish the job with 60-grit sandpaper on a random-orbital sander.

If you are making a new transom plate, do so before the canvas is stretched onto the canoe. The new marine plywood (or solid hardwood, if you refer) will be cut to a rough shape, then attached to the transom for the

final grinding and sanding. This is best done when there is no canvas to ruin.

To get the rough shape of the transom plate, clamp the new plywood to the transom with a finished edge flush to the top of the transom. Use a permanent-ink marker and draw the rough outline of the plate. Remove the plywood and cut the piece to a rough shape with a sabre saw or band saw.

Drill and counter-sink a series of pilot holes for the 1" (25 mm) #8 silicon bronze wood screws that will secure the plate against the transom.

(Above) Use the original transom plate as a template to draw a rough outline of the new plate onto a new board.

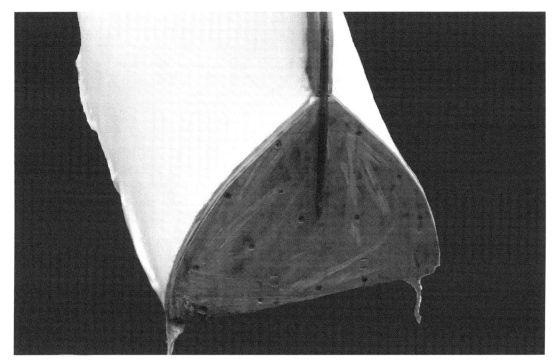

(Left) Secure the transom plate to the transom with a series of #8 silicon bronze wood screws. The plate is sealed with marine bedding compound.

(Top right) Somehow a loose tack got trapped between the canvas and the canoe. It can be removed without removing the canvas from the canoe.

(Bottom right) A pair of long-handled forceps can reach a loose tack (or other debris) before it drops too far into the space between the canvas and the canoe.

(Left) A strip of thin ash is used to push debris out of the space between the canvas and the canoe.

Trouble-shooting

Everything has gone according to plan. You have stretched the new canvas on to your canoe and tacked it snug along the sheer line. When you turn the canoe over, you discover a tack (or some other debris) has managed to end up trapped between the canoe and the new canvas.

This has happened more than once in my shop. The first thing that comes to mind (after a string of four-letter words) is the prospect of removing half the tacks in order to get at the debris. However, I have discovered that an ounce of prevention is worth a pound of cure. I have taken to keeping a pair of long-handled forceps on hand to retrieve any tacks that happen to drop between the canvas and the canoe. With them, I'm able to grab the tack without lifting the canvas away from the canoe. However, despite all of the precautions, you may still end up with something trapped under the canvas in a spot that seems impossible to get at.

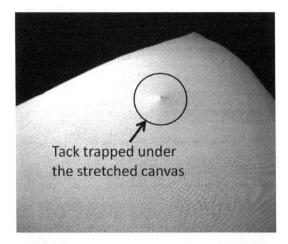

Tack trapped under the stretched canvas

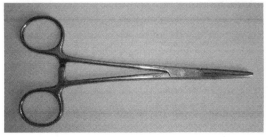

I'm sure most builders/restorers have their own ways of clearing this debris. Here is how I do it. First, make a tool for the job. Cut a 6' (180 cm) strip of ash 1¼" (32 mm) wide and 3/32" (2.5 mm) thick. Ash this thin flexes very well and is still strong enough to handle the stress. Cut a concave notch across the width of the strip at one end to create the "working" end. Round off any sharp edges with sandpaper and you have your own "Under-Canvas Debris Cleaner".

Remove three or four tacks on each side of the canoe in line with the debris. Create an opening large enough to allow the Debris Cleaner to get in between the canvas and the canoe. Then feed the working end under the canvas. Use one hand to feed the Debris Cleaner ahead while the other hand keeps the working end flush with the hull of the canoe. Press the working end down against the canoe and push more of the strip in under the canvas. When you get to the offending object, make sure the Debris Cleaner is lined up with it. Continue to push the strip ahead until it comes out on the other side. Make sure the Debris Cleaner does not place undue stress on the canvas. Then, it is just a case of replacing six or eight tacks to "close the patient" and complete the operation.

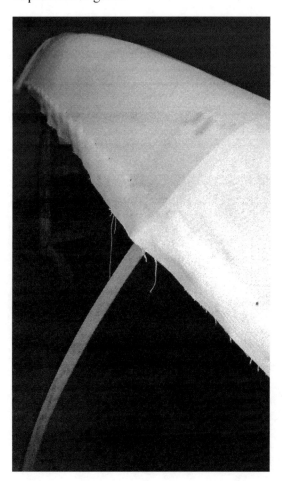

Canvas Filler

With the canvas on and the nap burned off, it is time to prepare the outside surface with a filler to make it waterproof. As with most things in a canoe restoration, there are options.

Oil-Based Filler

Historically, every canoe builder had their own recipe for canvas filler. This mixture creates a hard, flexible waterproof sizing for the canvas. Without it, the paint would soak into the canvas to make a very rough mess. In the early days, they used white lead – a mixture of lead carbonate and linseed oil – to create a lovely smooth surface. The one drawback is that white lead is highly toxic.

I am not keen on killing brain cells, so I opt for a recipe from the Wooden Canoe Heritage Association that uses silica and enamel instead of lead. The recipe is as follows:

* 43 oz. (1.2 litres) double-boiled linseed oil
* 21 oz. (590 ml) mineral spirits
* 34 oz. (950 ml) enamel
* 2 oz. (56 ml) Japan drier
* 2 oz. (56 ml) spar varnish
* 6.25 lbs. (2.8 kg) silica (300-325 mesh)

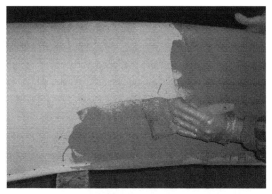

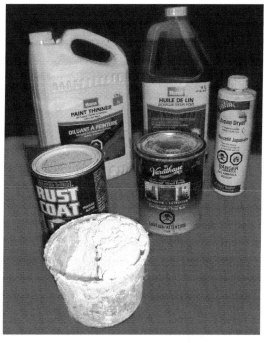

(Right) Paint thinner, linseed oil, Japan dryer, alkyd enamel, varnish and silica are mixed together to create an oil-based canoe canvas filler.

I use any alkyd enamel available at the local hardware store. It is strong and flexible and works very well in this application. A grey colour contrasts well against the canvas and allows me to see any spots I missed in the application. Silica (powdered glass) is available from pottery supply shops and is usually sold in a 325 mesh (a fine powder). Japan drier is a drying agent that helps the mixture dry quickly (one month at room temperature). Make sure you get boiled linseed oil. It's not actually boiled but rather it contains drying agents. Raw linseed oil takes forever to dry.

When mixing the ingredients, you may be surprised at the consistency. Many expect to be working with a thick putty-like substance. Instead, what you get, at first glance, is very thin and runny. However, when applied to the canvas, it is quite dense. Be sure to wear a good respirator when mixing the ingredients. Silica can cause silicosis if it gets into the lungs. I use a 4" brush and apply the filler to the canvas in small sections to maintain a wet edge as you work your way around the canoe. Stir the mixture between every brush-load to keep the silica suspended.

Apply enough filler to cover the weave of the canvas and move on to the next section. When you are finished, do a careful check and apply more filler to areas that were missed or less than completely filled.

(Top left) Apply oil-based canoe filler to the canvas with a 4" brush. Work in small sections to maintain a wet edge as you work around the canoe.

(Bottom left) Wait a few hours before smoothing the oil-based canvas filler by hand. A vinyl glove helps and keeps you a little cleaner.

Some oil-based fillers recommend two coats, but I find this formula works very well with a single coat. Some also recommend rubbing the filler into the weave with a canvas mitt. With this formula, I come back to the canoe about three or four hours later and use a vinyl glove on my hand to smooth out the filler before it has a chance to set up completely. The rough surface is made smooth.

Set the canoe aside and allow the filler to dry at room temperature for at least one month. Once dry, the filler is sanded with 220-grit sandpaper. The silica in the filler tends to polish to a smooth base for paint.

Water-Based Filler

If you would like a filler that dries in 30 hours instead of 30 days, there is an alternative.

In commercial and industrial buildings, air-duct systems used to be wrapped in asbestos. Now that this material is no longer used, the ducts are wrapped in canvas and sealed with a substance known as a "lagging compound" which is fire-resistant. It also contains fungicides to help prevent rot. It is specifically designed to waterproof canvas.

These lagging compounds are available through building supply companies under two brands: CHIL-SEAL® CP-50A MV1 and BAKOR® 120-09.

Both of these products are waterborne latex compounds. There are no nasty volatile organic compounds (VOC's) to contend with. Clean-up is accomplished with nothing more than a bucket of water. Most importantly, the drying time for this latex-based canvas filler is about 30 hours.

Start by getting a base coat on the canvas. Use a 6" (15 cm) foam roller to apply the filler to the canvas. Work on one small area (about 6' or two meters) at a time and proceed around the canoe until the first coat is applied.

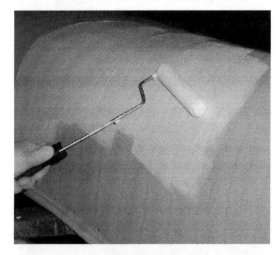

(Top left) Use a 6" (15 cm) foam roller to apply waterborne latex "Lagging Compound" to the canoe canvas. It is a great canoe canvas filler that dries in about two days.

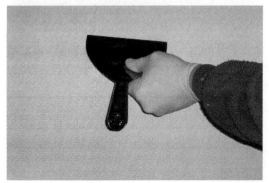

(Bottom left) Scrape excess lagging compound from the canvas with a 6" putty knife.

Once applied with the foam roller, use a 6" (15 cm) putty knife to remove excess compound and smooth the surface. Use only 3" of the 6" scraper to remove excess filler. This will prevent the filler from escaping around the edge of the scraper to form a ridge of filler. If an edge remains, use your hand to smooth the surface. This must be done immediately as the filler dries very quickly. You want to be able to smooth the compound before it sets up — we are talking about a matter of minutes, so there is no time to fuss and fret. Get it on, remove the excess along with any obvious ridges of filler on the canvas and move on to the next section. It is important to maintain a wet edge as you apply the compound from one section to the next, so keep moving. By the time you have worked your way around the entire canoe, it is time for the next coat. A minimum of three coats are required to fill the canvas to a smooth finish. Some people prefer four coats.

It takes the better part of a full day to complete the filling process. Then, just walk away and let the filler cure for a couple of days. Many people respond to my account of this process with: "There must be a catch. It can't be that easy." Well, if there is a catch, I haven't found it. It really is that easy.

Once dry, take down the rough spots with 120-grit sandpaper and a random-orbital sander. Unlike oil-based filler, this stuff does not polish. Sand lightly and quickly to smooth the surface. Now, your canoe is ready for paint.

Epoxy Filler

I have not tried using epoxy as a canvas filler, so I can only speak to my experience and understanding of this product in general as well as comments I have read on-line. Also, I have not restored a canoe that has an epoxy-impregnated canvas, so I don't know what problems, if any, this approach creates in the long term (i.e. twenty or thirty years).

It seems to me that the epoxy, being a plastic, would not allow the canvas to breathe and would hold water against the wood hull for extended periods. This warm, moist environment would be ideal for the growth of the fungi that cause rot. Therefore, the long-term health of the canoe would probably be jeopardized by an epoxy-impregnated canvas.

One thing that keeps me from experimenting with epoxy as a canvas filler is cost. Purchasing enough resin, hardener and fillers to fill a canoe canvas is more than double the cost of either an oil-based filler or a water-based filler. I am very happy with the way both of these fillers work, so I am not inclined to invest in a costly experiment when I see no reason to look for an alternative.

Another part of my reluctance in using epoxy for this purpose comes down to a question of compatability. For me, one of the things that makes a wood-canvas canoe so special is the fact that it moves and breathes as part its environment. Epoxies create a canvas that is hard and rigid while the rest of the canoe wants to give and flex. It would seem to me that a flexible canoe and a rigid canvas would not result in a happy marriage. My comments are not based on first-hand experience and should be taken with that in mind. If you decide to try using epoxy as a canvas filler, please let me know how it works for you, especially in the long term.

(Above) Sand the waterborne latex canoe canvas filler lightly with 120-grit sandpaper.

(Left) The canvas is filled, dried and sanded. This took a total of two days. If time is a consideration, choose latex canvas filler over the oil-based filler.

Alternatives to Canvas

Surely, with all the technological advances developed in the past hundred years, a covering for a wood-canvas canoe must have been invented that is more durable, easier to apply and simpler to maintain than traditional painted canvas.

Covering a canoe with canvas requires a lot of specialized skills and equipment. So, let's take a look at three alternatives.

Dacron

This is DuPont's trade name for its polyester fabric and tends to be used as a general term for any polyester fabric. It was developed in 1951 and offers a durable, rot-resistant, light-weight alternative to cotton in things such as small aircraft construction and sailboat sails. I have only used it once to restore a Peterborough Model 44 sailing canoe. It works very well for sails. I have not used it as an alternative to the canvas covering on the hull, so I will limit my comments to a couple of key points.

Polyester fibers do not stretch. Therefore, it cannot be pulled tightly over the compound curves of a canoe. Instead, it is heat-shrunk onto the hull. Since U.V. radiation (sunlight) breaks down polyester very quickly, the fabric must be protected before it is filled and painted.

Although polyester has good abrasion resistance, its main drawback is a lack of tear resistance. Because polyester fibers do not stretch, tearing forces tend to be handled one fiber at a time rather than sharing the force across many fibers as happens with canvas. Therefore, when a tearing force is strong enough to break one fiber, it is strong enough to break all of the fibers. It happens so fast, it's referred to as 'explosive tearing'.

Since polyester fabric is heat-shrunk onto a canoe, every little flaw shows through. The hull of a restored canoe is rarely, if ever, flawless. Therefore, polyester fabric would be better suited for new construction. It also offers very little protection to the wood. Where canvas cushions the blow to some degree, polyester does not.

It seems that polyester is a viable alternative to canvas – with some significant caveats:

a) A tear in polyester fabric is catastrophic
b) Every flaw in the hull will show through
c) Any blows to the hull are not cushioned.

Dacron works very well as a fabric for canoe sails. However, as an alternative to a canvas covering for canoes, it has several limitations.

Tremblay canoes used vinyl-impregnated canvas to cover their canoes in the 1970's and 1980's. Canoe restorers now find extensive rot in canoe hulls where the "plastic bag" kept the wood moist for extended periods. (Tremblay Canoes catalogue cover circa 1970.)

Vinyl-Impregnated Canvas

Canoe builders have used vinyl-impregnated (PVC-coated) canvas since the 1970's. Verolite was one of the original brands. While builders continue to use it, most professional canoe restorers exchange horror stories with each other about the rotted canoe hulls they have found when they removed 30-year-old vinyl-impregnated canvas from canoes that would have been fine otherwise. Consequently, most canoe restorers I have met refuse to use it.

The concerns I mentioned earlier about using epoxy as a canvas filler (page 109) stem from what I have seen in canoes covered with vinyl-impregnated canvas. It acts as a big plastic bag and holds water against the hull for extended periods. After 30 or 40 years, it is removed to find the hull almost completely rotted. Regular painted canvas breathes and allows water to evaporate quickly – if the canoe is stored correctly.

Another consideration is that the vinyl tends not to accept paint very well. I'm guessing there is some kind of paint that will adhere to the vinyl, but I doubt it would work in the context of a wood-canvas canoe.

It appears that vinyl-impregnated canvas is convenient to use because there is no filler to mix, no drying time required and no need to spend a week or more applying paint. It is durable and is lighter than painted canvas. However, most canoes covered with it that have been used regularly for many years tend to arrive in the restoration shop as one big mass of rotted wood. Therefore, vinyl-impregnated canvas appears to create huge headaches in the long term.

Fiberglass

If you haven't guessed already, let me go on the record as saying that I am dead-set against the idea of fiberglass on a wood-canvas canoe. It is not that I am a purist. Instead, for me, it is a matter of repairability. As soon as you apply epoxy resin (the stuff that binds the fiberglass to the hull), the ability to repair it is reduced to somewhere between difficult and impossible.

To anyone considering putting fiberglass on a wood-canvas canoe, my question is, "What are you trying to achieve by doing this?" Many people have the impression that these canoes are delicate or fragile. They believe that something must be done to make them stronger and more durable. Yes, with fiberglass on your canoe you can run it up on the beach and not worry about getting your feet wet. However, a wood-canvas canoe is anything but fragile and can take a lot of rough treatment over the years. By putting fiberglass on your canoe, you actually decrease its durability. When it comes time to fix the canoe (and that time will certainly come), unless the restorer is willing to devote weeks to the removal of the epoxy, it will end up in the landfill. How durable is that?

Another common reason for considering fiberglass cloth instead of canvas is know-how. Many people view fiberglass as easier to apply and I suppose they are right. Again, I come back to my original question, "What are you trying to achieve?" If you want your canoe to last virtually forever, it seems worthwhile to learn how to canvas your canoe. With a "traditional" painted canvas cover, your canoe remains infinitely repairable.

While fiberglass can be applied without an elaborate set-up and a huge learning curve, you are sacrificing the long-term life of the canoe for the sake of some convenience in the shop and dry feet on a canoe trip. Personally, I view learning how to canvas a canoe as a step towards helping to make it live forever. When I am paddling, I am prepared to get my feet wet while I carry my canoe from the water to the beach. It seems like a small price to pay.

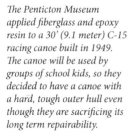

The Penticton Museum applied fiberglass and epoxy resin to a 30' (9.1 meter) C-15 racing canoe built in 1949. The canoe will be used by groups of school kids, so they decided to have a canoe with a hard, tough outer hull even though they are sacrificing its long term repairability.

8

Keel and Stem-bands

S tem-bands are metal strips installed at each end of the canoe to protect the canvas seam. They have a very specific and undeniable function. The keel, on the other hand, is a controversial topic. Is it necessary on a wood-canvas canoe (or any canoe for that matter)? We will start this chapter with that burning question. We will then get into the specifics of making and installing these components.

The Keel Question
If there is an area of controversy in the world of wood-canvas canoes, the question of the keel would be it.

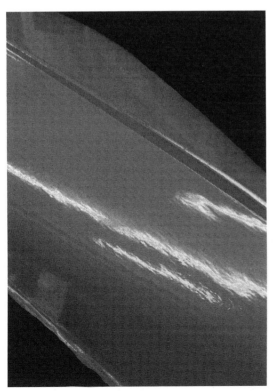

Historically
In days gone by, North American canoes did not have keels. Edwin Tappen Adney documented hundreds of indigenous water craft in the book *Bark Canoes and Skin Boats of North America*. They ranged from small hunting canoes around 11' (3.35 meters) long to large cargo canoes over 36' (11 meters) long. None of them had a keel.

As people of European ancestry started building canoes in the 1800's, they tended to approach the task from a European perspective. They started building a boat by setting up a keelson. The rest of the vessel is built around it. As canoes became a commodity for the general public, canoe builders also had to appeal to a market that didn't trust a boat without a keel. Many people unfamiliar with canoes feel unstable in them and have trouble travelling in a straight line. As a result, most canoes sold in the better part of the 20th century were equipped with a keel. However, it is interesting to note that true working canoes built at the same time (such as the Chestnut Prospector, Cruiser and Ogilvy) were usually keel-free.

(Left) Bill Greenwood built about 300 canoes a year in Richmond, BC. He stated unequivocally, "My canoes have keels."

(Rightt) The Chestnut Ogilvy has a wide, flat-bottom hull to make it slow and stable in the water.

Stability

The Chestnut Ogilvy was designed by and for professional fishing guides in New Brunswick. They would stand up in the canoe all day long and pole upstream while their clients fished for salmon in the shallow, rapid rivers. A true working river canoe, the Ogilvy never had a keel. Its wide, flat bottom gave the canoe great stability.

Wider canoes – 36" (90 cm) or more – with flat bottoms tend to have greater "initial stability" than narrow canoes – 34" (85 cm) or less – with arched bottoms. What is gained in stability with a wide, flat bottom is lost in hull speed, and conversely, what is gained in hull speed with a narrow, arched bottom is lost in stability. Attaching a strip of wood an inch high to the bottom of a canoe does little to affect stability one way or the other.

The Chestnut Prospector was designed to dance around rocks in rapid rivers. Although it has a more rounded bottom than the Ogilvy, the tumblehome and high sides in the centre give it very good "secondary" stability. This means when it is tipped over on one side, it becomes stable in that position. Also, the waterline width increases as more weight is loaded into the canoe. Greater width at the water-line equals more stability.

Tracking

The ability of a canoe to travel in a straight line (or "track") is a function of its waterline length. Note here that I refer specifically to the waterline length rather than the canoe's length overall. The hull of a Chestnut Prospector lifts dramatically at the ends. As a result, an unloaded 16' (4.9 meters) canoe will only be about 13' (4 meters) long at the waterline. What is lost in tracking with a shorter waterline length is gained in maneuverability; the converse is also true: what is gained in tracking with longer waterline length is lost in maneuverability.   When some people think of a canoe that tracks well, they think of a canoe with a keel. In fact, a keel is of little consequence when it comes to tracking. If you are simply looking for a canoe that will travel in a straight line, get a long canoe – 17' (5.2 meters) or more – with no rocker.

Functionally, many canoes are designed to navigate rivers. The rivers of northern Canada are typically fast and deep with lots of large rocks. Pleasure canoes built by the Chestnut and Peterborough Canoe companies were equipped with a "shoe" keel. At 3/8" (9 mm) high and 2¼" (57 mm) wide, it provided protection to the bottom without interfering with the canoe's ability to sideslip past rocks in rapid rivers.

(Left) The Chestnut Prospector has a narrow (compared to the Ogilvy), arched-bottom hull to make it fast and maneuverable in the water.

Handling Wind

In lakes, many people complain that a canoe without a keel will be blown around by the wind. Again, it comes back to learning how to handle the canoe. When travelling on a large lake with the wind in your face, the canoe must be loaded with the majority of the weight in the forward half of the canoe. It will always tend to "weather-vein" – that is, it will orient itself with the lighter end downwind. As long as the weight is upwind, the canoe will not spin around as you paddle into the wind.

Design vs Tradition

If the question of keels in canoes was strictly one of form and function, there would not be a discussion. You only have to look at any modern Royalex or Kevlar canoe on the market. None of the canoes built today have keels – and rightly so. However, in the world of wood-canvas canoes, there is more to consider. Many people have grown up with their canoes. It is part of their life and part of their family. Their canoe has had a keel for fifty years, so it seems only natural that it stays that way. In this context I say, "Fair enough." It turns out that wood-canvas canoes are more than form and function. They must be seen in the context of family history and tradition. For this reason, I have no problem re-installing a keel in a wood-canvas canoe.

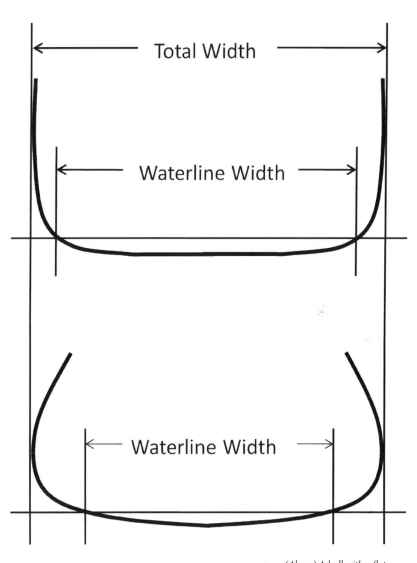

(Above) A hull with a flat bottom and straight sides (top) is wide at the water-line when loaded lightly. By comparison, a hull with an arched bottom and tumblehome (bottom) is narrow at the water-line when loaded lightly.

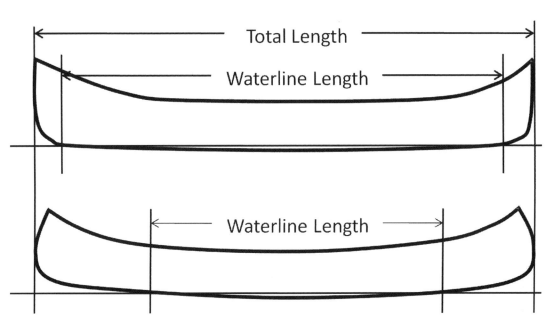

(Left) A hull with little rocker (top) has most of its total length touching the water making it harder to turn. By comparison, a hull with substantial rocker (bottom) has much less of its total length touching the water, thus making it harder to keep going in a straight line.

Repairing a Keel

Most canoe keels are tapered at each end to a fine, thin tip. It is not uncommon for this tip to break off at some point before the keel is re-installed.

Begin the repair by turning the canoe upside-down and placing the keel in its original position. At the undamaged end of the canoe, measure the distance from the end of the canoe to the tip of the keel. Transfer this measurement to the other end and mark the final length of the keel on the bottom of the canoe at the damaged end.

Mark a 6:1 scarf angle on the damaged end of the keel and measure the distance from the start of the scarf joint to the point marked on the canoe that indicates the final length of the repaired keel. This will give you a rough idea of how much wood to use in your repair. Add about 6" (15 cm) to that length and select a piece of hardwood for the repair.

Cut the scarf angle into the keel at the damaged end. Then, sand it flush and smooth. Measure the height and width of the keel at the beginning of the scarf joint and cut the new wood to those dimensions. Transfer the scarf angle from the keel to the new wood and cut the scarf angle. Be sure the new wood is at least 6" (15 cm) longer than required.

Assemble the repair and glue it with polyurethane glue. Let it cure overnight, then sand the joint smooth.

Position the keel on the canoe again and mark the final length onto the new wood. Cut the keel to its final length. Use the taper at the undamaged end as a template and mark it into the new wood at the repaired end.

Shape the taper. I use an angle grinder set up with a 24-grit sanding disc for the rough shaping and finish it to 80-grit with a random-orbital sander.

Making a Keel

The keel is a simple structure. There are usually no real surprises or difficulties to be aware of in this process.

Turn the canoe upside-down and mark a position approximately 16" (40 cm) from the end of the canoe along the centre-line at each end. Measure from the mark at one end to the mark at the other end to determine the length of the keel. It is usually longer than a single hardwood board, so your stock will probably have to be scarfed together to make a full-length piece.

Once you have a full length piece of hardwood, cut it to the dimensions of the original keel. Then, mark out a long, gradual taper at both ends. The keel tapers both in height and width. Use the original keel as a template or refer to the dimensions presented in Chapter 12 as a guide. Shape the ends with an angle grinder and a random-orbital sander. Sand it smooth with 80-grit sandpaper.

(Left) New wood is glued to the original keel with polyurethane glue.

(Right) The new keel tip is shaped and sanded smooth to create an exact copy of the original tip.

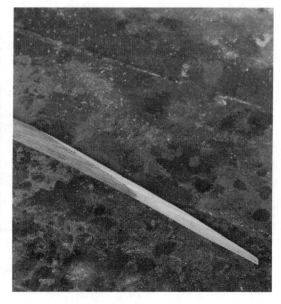

Installing a Keel

Most keels are removed at the beginning of the restoration project and need to be re-installed. Therefore, the first step is to clean it and remove old paint and bedding compound. This is usually a two-step process. Start with an angle grinder set up with a 24-grit sanding disk. This cuts through the worst of the old material and gets down to the original wood. Care must be taken in order to remove only the old paint and bedding compound. Finish the job with a random-orbital sander set up with 80-grit sandpaper. This removes any marks made by the grinder and creates a smooth surface for new bedding compound and paint.

Having just spent a lot of time and effort creating a waterproof canvas cover, it seems a little strange to then poke a dozen or more holes through the bottom of the canoe. It is essential, therefore, to use a bedding compound that creates a seal that stays waterproof and flexible for decades.

Most canoes use 1" (25 mm) #6 flat head silicon bronze screws combined with brass finish washers. Turn the canoe on its edge to allow access to both the interior and exterior at the same time. Clamp the inwale of the canoe to the canoe cradle with a spring clamp to hold it in place. Begin by driving one screw into each end of the canoe from the inside.

With one screw at each end, move to the outside of the canoe and line up each screw with the original holes in the keel. Use a permanent-ink marker to show the position of the keel on the canvas.

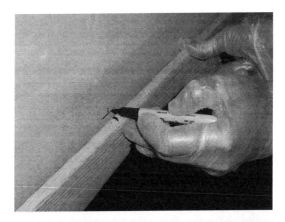
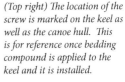

(Top right) The location of the screw is marked on the keel as well as the canoe hull. This is for reference once bedding compound is applied to the keel and it is installed.

(Bottom right) Drive a screw through the canvas from the interior as a starting point for the keel installation. Start with one screw at either end as well as one screw near the centre of the canoe.

Apply bedding compound generously to the keel with a putty knife. Any excess will be cleaned up later. For now, it is more important to ensure a good seal along the entire length of the keel. Then, clear away some of the compound covering the screw holes at each end in order to make it easier to find them.

Not everyone has my "wingspan" – 79" (200 cm) from finger-tip to finger-tip – so not everyone can hold the keel in place with one hand and drive the screw with the other. Get someone to help you line up the original holes in the keel with the screws. Sometimes the original holes in the keel have been stripped. Use 1" (25 mm) #8 screws to secure the keel. If the keel has warped a little, you may need 1¼" (32 mm) screws to draw it tight to the canoe. In this situation, especially with Chestnut and Peterborough shoe keels (3/8" thick), the screws may go right through the keel and poke out on the outer surface. That will be dealt with later.

(Left) It helps to have long arms when you are installing a keel without assistance. It is much easier to ask for some help.

117

Once the keel is attached at both the bow and the stern, check to make sure the keel is straight down the centre-line of the canoe. Once aligned, drive the rest of the screws along its full length. Usually, it is necessary to apply some pressure on the keel in order for the screws to catch properly. Sometimes I need to get under seats to drive the screws. This is where a flexible drill extension comes in very handy. Otherwise, remove the seats to give free access to the centre-line of the canoe.

Remove excess bedding compound from the edges of the keel and apply more to areas that are not completely sealed. Remove any bedding compound stuck to the canvas with medium steel wool soaked in lacquer thinner.

Use a file to take care of any screw-tips poking through the keel. Finally, let the bedding compound cure for a few days before applying paint.

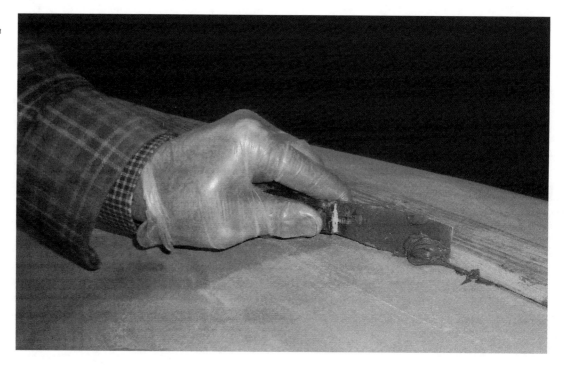

Making Stem-bands

Stem-bands are usually strips of half-oval metal. They protect the canvas seam along the outside face of the stems. Most often, they are made of brass, but I have seen copper and aluminum used as well. When the original stem-bands are broken or missing, new ones need to be made and installed.

Often you are able to remove the originals when the old canvas is removed and re-install them once the new canvas is attached and filled. Some people install the stem-bands after the canvas is painted. I prefer to install them before painting in order to get a better seal between the brass and the canvas.

Original brass stem-bands are often made of naval brass and therefore, tend to be harder, heavier and more likely to break when bent around the curves of the stem. The metal is very thin around the drilled and counter-sunk holes, so original stem-bands are easy to break. Care must be taken when handling them.

The length of the stem-band varies with each canoe, but they tend to be between 36" and 48" (90 cm and 120 cm) long. Since the brass usually comes in lengths of 6' (180 cm) or more, the first step is to measure the canoe-end, determine the length needed and cut the brass to length.

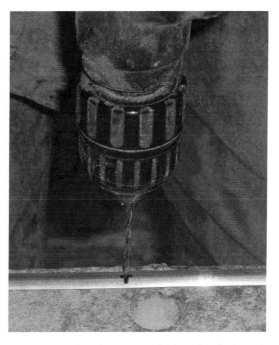

(Right) Drill a pilot hole in the brass stem-band. A sharp bit and low RPMs are essential.

Many stem-bands are attached to the deck and bend around the stem-end before continuing along the outer face of the stem to protect the canvas seam. Position the brass on the deck of the canoe and mark the location of the screw-hole as well as the bend at the stem-end.

The location of the first screw on the stem is a few inches below the stem-top. The rest of the screws along the stem-band are spaced about 6" (15 cm) apart. Position these holes by eye along the length of the stem-band. There is nothing critical about the screw locations as long as they are fairly evenly spaced.

Some restorers use a drill press to make the screw-holes, and some go so far as to make custom centering jigs for the job. I opt to do it by eye with a hand drill. The trick is to use a sharp drill bit and to keep the revolutions-per-minute very low.

Counter-sink the screw-holes with the appropriate size of counter-sink bit. This job requires some care and attention. Since the metal is fairly soft, it is easy to punch right through it, creating a huge hole in the stem-band. Yes, this is the voice of experience speaking.

(Left) Countersink the stem-band holes with a dedicated tool for countersinking metal.

119

Round off the end of the stem-band that attaches to the deck. Then, file the bottom end to a shallow chamfer. This can be done with a good file, but I make short work of the job with an angle grinder and a very light touch.

The bend at the stem-end is best done by heating the brass with a propane torch. The angle of the bend is taken from the canoe with a sliding bevel. Clamp the brass into a metal vise with the bending point about 1" (2.5 cm) outside the jaws of the vise. After heating for about a minute, the brass begins to bend easily. Apply slow, steady pressure until the required amount of bend is achieved. The brass can break if the bend is made too quickly, so take your time. Check the bend with the sliding bevel and continue bending until you've got what you want. Then quench the brass in cold water.

The rest of the stem-band is bent in a similar way using the propane torch until it fits the shape of the canoe stem. The stem-bands are now ready for installation.

Installing Stem-bands

If you are re-installing original stem-bands, start by pre-fitting them. They ought to sit nicely in place. However, if the stem-band has been kinked or requires substantial bending, use a propane torch to heat the metal before it is shaped to fit. Once the stem-band is back to the desired form, quench it with lots of water.

If the stem-bands attach to the decks, cut the canvas back from the stem at the top of the planking. This gives you access to the stem-top. I put a new blade in my utility knife and cut back about 2" (5 cm).

Apply bedding compound evenly to the inside surface of the stem-band with a putty knife. This seals the area and prevents water from leaking in through the holes drilled along the stem. Apply it right up to the top of the stem leaving bare the section of stem-band that runs from the stem-top to the deck.

Centre the end of the stem-band on the deck and drill a pilot hole for the screw. Attach the top end of the stem-band to the deck. It may help to make a test hole in a scrap piece of hardwood to ensure that it is the correct size. If the hole is too small, the silicon-bronze screws will heat up and snap off as you attempt to screw them into the wood; too large, and the screws will pull out. Reduce the amount of heat generated by the friction of bronze against hardwood with a little penetrating oil sprayed into the pilot hole.

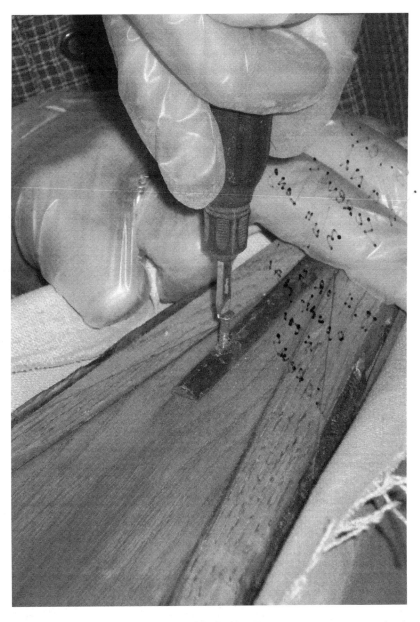

(Above) Attach the stem-band to the deck.

(Left) Apply marine bedding compound liberally to the stem-band.

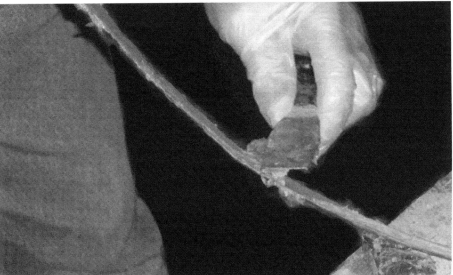

(Top right) Seat the stem-band against the stem with a mallet.

As you attach the stem-band, centre it on the stem. Use a wooden mallet to flatten the band against the stem. Since the stem-band has been pre-fit, the amount of cold bending required at this stage is of little concern.

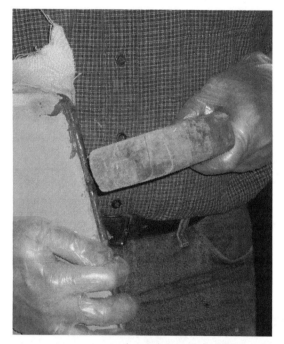

For each fastener along the stem-band, pre-drill a pilot hole and screw it into place. From time to time, you may encounter a brass tack along the stem. If so, drill through it with low rpm's. Then continue with the regular drill speed. For most locations along the stem-band, the screws are ¾" (19 mm) long. Along the bottom of the canoe, you may feel the drill hit a space between the canvas and the stem. In this case, use a 1" (25 mm) screw.

When the entire stem-band is attached, use more bedding compound to fill any gaps. Then scrape away excess compound. Clean up the canvas and brass with medium steel wool soaked in lacquer thinner

(Bottom right) Drill a pilot hole for each screw in the stem-band before driving the screw.

If you want to show off the brass once the canoe is completed, scrape the paint from the stem-bands with a utility knife the day after the final coat of paint is applied. This will also remove any old paint or tarnish from the brass. If you attempt to clean the brass before it is installed on the canoe, there is a good chance you will break the stem-band (first-hand experience again).

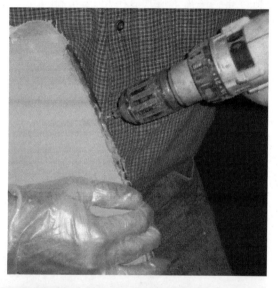

Use extra fine steel wool to polish the brass. Paint that is scuffed around the stem-bands can be touched up with a little extra paint and an artist's brush.

(Bottom) You have the option to expose the brass stem-bands after the paint has been applied. It makes for a pretty detail in the overall project.

Handwritten notes in margin: stem band screws 3/4" Long NO. 4 or 5 Round head wood screws

9
Paint and Varnish

This is what you have all been waiting for. Applying paint and varnish is one of the most satisfying jobs in the entire restoration project. When a client asks me to restore their canoe, they occasionally want to "do the finish work" themselves. Although painting and varnishing are less demanding technically and do not require a lot of specialized tools, the process is not without its challenges. Therefore, when someone asks to apply the paint and varnish, I respectfully decline their request. When people see a fully restored canoe, they are drawn immediately to the finish work. A first class job in everything else means nothing if the quality of the paint and varnish is sub-standard. So, here is how to get a professional look in your paint and varnish.

Professional results are not difficult to achieve once you know how oil-based paint and varnish work.

Apply a coat of paint to the filled canvas while a coat of varnish is drying.

Basic Approach

As mentioned in Chapter 1, alkyd enamel (paint) and spar varnish are both oil-based and, as such, are handled in very much the same way. The only significant difference between the two from a preparation perspective is that you wet sand between coats of paint and dry sand (with either sandpaper or steel wool) between coats of varnish. With that in mind, I will describe how to prepare and apply paint. I will not go into detail when discussing varnish since most of it is the same as paint. Shellac has its own methods for preparation and application, so these will be discussed in a separate section.

In terms of the order of events, some people prefer to shellac and varnish the interior before stretching the canvas. It is just a matter of personal preference. I choose to canvas the canoe, install the keel and stembands and then tackle the paint and varnish. While a coat of paint is drying on the canvas exterior, I apply a coat of spar varnish to the interior. Then, while the spar varnish is drying, I apply the next coat of paint. My schedule is as follows:

Day 1) First coat of paint
Day 2) Two coats of shellac
Day 2) First coat of varnish
Day 3) Second coat of paint
Day 4) Second coat of varnish
Day 5) Third coat of paint
Day 6) Third coat of varnish (if desired)
Day 7) Fourth coat of paint (if desired)
Day 8) Let it dry
Day 9) A coat of carnauba wax
Day 9) Final assembly of the canoe
Day 9) Final paint and varnish touch-ups

Paint

Sanding

Generally speaking, the quality of your sanding job is more important than the quantity. There is no need to spend hours sanding between each coat of paint. However, the more meticulous you are, the better the end results. Before starting to paint the filled canvas, sand the filler with 120-grit sandpaper. I use a random-orbital sander for this job.

Any tacks in the canoe hull that are not flush to the hull will show up as you sand. It is essential to stop sanding immediately and re-clinch the tack to avoid creating a nice, round, tack-sized hole in the canvas. If you do sand through the canvas, use a little two-part epoxy putty to fill the hole. Once it has hardened, sand the filler smooth (gentle hand sanding).

Use 120-grit dry sandpaper (random-orbital sander) between the first and second coats of paint. Use 220-grit wet sandpaper (hand sanding) between the second and third coats. Use 320-grit wet sandpaper (hand sanding) between the third and fourth coats. Clean the surfaces well before applying the paint. Remove sanding dust with a brush or vacuum. Then, wipe away remaining dust with a tack cloth.

Thinning

Some articles about oil-based paints and varnishes would have you believe that avoiding streaks and bubbles in the final finish is one of life's great challenges. In fact, there is no great mystery to it. Thin the paint (or varnish) about 12% with mineral spirits (paint thinner) before using it. The thinned paint will self-level once it is applied. The additional solvent also allows the paint to dry before sags and drips develop.

Here's an easy way to thin paint about 12%: When you buy a gallon (4 litres) of paint, pick up an empty can at the same time. When you are ready to apply the paint, pour 2 cups (500 ml) of paint thinner into the empty can. Pour the paint from its original container into the new can containing the thinner. Pour the contents from the new can back to the original can. Do this a number of times until the paint and thinner are mixed thoroughly.

(Above) Use a random-orbital sander with 120-grit paper to prepare the surface of the canvas for the second coat of paint.

(Middle) Hand-sand with 220-grit wet sandpaper between the second and third coats of paint. Use 320-grit between the third and fourth coats.

(Below) Clinch any tacks that show through after sanding.

Apply the third and fourth coats of paint with a disposable foam brush.

Application

Use a high-quality 3" (75 mm) natural bristle brush to apply the first two coats of paint. For the third and fourth coats, use a 3" (75 mm) disposable foam brush. Pour a small amount of thinned paint from the original can into the new can. Load the brush by holding it vertically. Lower it into the paint until about two-thirds of the bristle length is submerged. Then, extract the brush from the paint, but before removing it from the can, rattle it against the sides of the can to remove excess paint. Hold the brush with the handle between your thumb and index finger. Place your finger tips on the metal base. Holding a paint brush is similar to holding a pencil.

Work in a space with lots of air circulation. Be sure that the space is well lit - preferably from an angle. As you apply the paint, position the newly painted surface between you and the light. Check for any missed spots by looking for reflections of the light on the wet surface. Apply the paint with the brush held at a 45° angle to the surface. Brush on the paint hard and rub it in to make sure it spreads evenly. This is done quickly and vigorously. Don't worry about streaks or bubbles; they will disappear on their own.

Start on one side of the canoe at one end and apply paint to a small section. As soon as the paint is spread evenly, use the ends of the brush bristles to "tip" the newly painted surface. This is done twice. First, tip vertically from the centre-line of the canoe to the sheer-line. Move over slightly after each stroke until the entire section has been done. Second, tip horizontally starting at the centre-line and moving down slightly after each stroke until you reach the sheer-line. The "tipping" strokes are very light and very quick. Then, load the brush again, move over to the next small section of canvas and repeat the process. It is important to maintain a "wet edge" as you work around the canoe, so apply paint to small sections and be sure to overlap the brush strokes. Once you have applied paint to the entire canvas, go around the canoe again looking for any drips (usually at the ends) or areas where too much paint was applied. Use your brush (not loaded with paint) to spread the paint more thoroughly and re-tip it. All of the paint application is done quickly. It will take about 30 or 40 minutes to apply a coat of paint to the entire canvas. Leave the paint alone to dry for 48 hours. It will be dry enough after 24 hours to turn the canoe right-side up and apply a coat of varnish to the exposed wood.

Clean up

Use the brush to remove paint from the gutter of the paint can. Place the lid back on the can and place an old rag on top of the lid. Use a rubber mallet to close the lid tightly to the can. The rag will prevent any paint left in the gutter from splashing all over the shop.

Natural bristle brushes are cleaned in three stages. First, clean with mineral spirits (paint thinner). Then, clean with lacquer thinner. Finally, clean the brushes with a heavy duty cleaner such as Lestoil®.

Shellac

Sanding

Use extra fine steel wool to buff shellac between coats as well as to prepare the shellacked surface for varnish. It buffs quickly and creates a great base for varnish. Vacuum the canoe to remove any debris. It would be nice to wipe away any other dust with a tack cloth, but it is difficult since the cloth often snags on the rough edges in the interior of the canoe.

Thinning

Shellac flakes are typically sold in one-pound bags which are then dissolved in denatured alcohol (also called methanol or methyl hydrate). The other option is to buy pre-mixed shellac from the hardware store. The concentration of shellac in the alcohol is referred to as the 'cut'. Pre-mixed shellac at the hardware store is typically a 'four-pound cut' – four pounds of shellac flakes dissolved in one gallon of alcohol. If you are dissolving shellac flakes, use alcohol to create a four-pound cut. This is a rather thick mix. Most woodworkers prefer a two-pound cut. Also, as mentioned in Chapter 1, shellac mixed in alcohol will turn cloudy if it comes into contact with water. To avoid this, dilute the four-pound cut of shellac with lacquer thinner. This creates a mixture that is often called lacquer. It will not become cloudy when exposed to water.

To dissolve shellac flakes in alcohol, place the flakes and enough alcohol for a four-pound cut into a clean one-gallon (4 liter) paint can. Close the lid tight and allow the

(Right) Scratch the surface of existing varnish with extra-fine steel wool to prepare it for the next coat of varnish.

mixture to sit overnight. Once you have the four-pound cut of shellac (either pre-mixed from the store or mixed from flakes), pour one quart (one liter) of shellac into a clean one gallon (4 liter) paint can and add one quart (one liter) of lacquer thinner. Mix it well with a stir stick.

Application

Use a high quality 2" (50 mm) natural bristle brush to apply two coats of shellac to all of the bare, exposed wood in the canoe. That includes all of the surfaces of the outwales. This stuff dries almost immediately, so application is fast and indelicate. Apply lots of shellac to a small area to ensure full coverage with one brush stroke. Shellac is more slopped on than painted on. Once applied, do not go over an area again. Simply apply one sloppy brush stroke and move over to the next small area. It is important to maintain a wet edge as you move down the length of the canoe, so speed is the key. Allow the shellac to dry for a couple of hours.

(Bottom) Shellac creates a beautiful base for varnish. It is easy to apply, dries in a couple of hours and polishes quickly with fine steel wool.

(Top) Apply spar varnish evenly and vigourously. Streaks and bubbles will self-level.

Varnish

Sanding
Prepare the exposed wood in the canoe for a coat of varnish the same way you did for a coat of shellac. Use extra fine steel wool and vacuum the surfaces to remove any debris. You are simply scratching the surfaces to allow the varnish to adhere well to the surface.

Application
Use a high quality 2" (50 mm) natural bristle brush to apply two coats of varnish to all of the exposed wood in the canoe. That includes all of the surfaces of the outwales. The application method is the same as for paint except it is difficult to tip the surfaces in both directions. Therefore, tip the interior in the direction that follows the direction of

the wood grain in the ribs. Tip the outwales in the direction of the wood grain as well (lengthwise). Spread the varnish evenly and thoroughly. Too much varnish applied to a section of the canoe's interior will pool in the bottom. Once you have applied varnish to the entire interior, use a 3" (75 mm) foam brush to soak up any pools of excess varnish. Then, tip the varnish on the decks and thwarts with the foam brush. Leave the varnish alone to dry for 48 hours. It will be dry enough after 24 hours to turn the canoe upside-down and apply a coat of paint to the canvas.

Wax
Once the final coat of paint has dried for at least 48 hours, apply a coat of carnauba wax. It will protect the paint for the first few months as it cures completely to a rock-hard finish.

(Bottom) Protect the painted surface with a coat of carnauba wax. Use lots of clean rags to polish the wax.

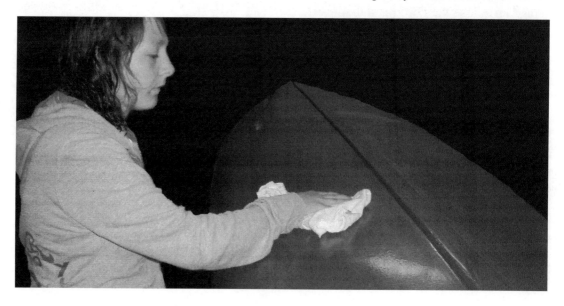

10
Final Assembly

T he marathon has been run and it is time to cross the finish line. Everything (or almost everything) is made and varnished. All of your hard work is rewarded as all of the pieces are assembled and your canoe truly comes back to life. Be prepared to shed a few tears as you stand back to see your canoe looking (and smelling) the way it did when you were ten years old. One client brought his two young boys into the shop to see their fully restored canoe. He turned to them and said, "Can you smell the varnish on the canoe? That smell gets into your soul and never leaves."

Assembling all the final pieces to complete the canoe is both satisfying and exciting.

Outwales

If you have followed the procedures outlined so far, most of the wood surfaces that would otherwise be susceptible to rot are now sealed. This alone will extend the life of your canoe. Some builders, like Jack Hurley in Dwight, Ontario, even apply varnish to the cut edge of the canvas before the outwales are attached.

(Top right) Trim the canvas along the top-edge of the planking with a utility knife.

Once the new canvas is painted and waxed, put a new blade into your utility knife and trim the canvas flush with the top of the planking. In most canoes, this is ½" below the rib-tops. Make sure you don't cut more than that. The outwales must cover the cut edge of the canvas, so take your time doing this. It is very easy to cut the canvas below the top of the sheer-line planking, so err on the side of caution the first time around the canoe by cutting high and then trim exactly the second time around.

If you are installing new outwales, put small pieces of masking tape on the top surface of the inwales to mark the locations of the screws that will hold the outwales to the canoe. A screw is driven into every second rib-top except at the ends where every rib has a screw. Mark the screw locations ahead of time to speed up the process later. It also ensures that the screw locations are the same on both sides of the canoe.

(Bottom right) Indicate the location of each screw in the outwale by placing a small piece of masking tape on the inwale at each position.

Make sure the outwale will cover the entire side of the canoe once it is in place. Clamp the outwale at the centre. Then, use a hardwood mallet to tap the outwale so that the top surface is flush with that of the inwale.

(Below) Use a mallet to tap the outwale until it is flush with the rib-tops.

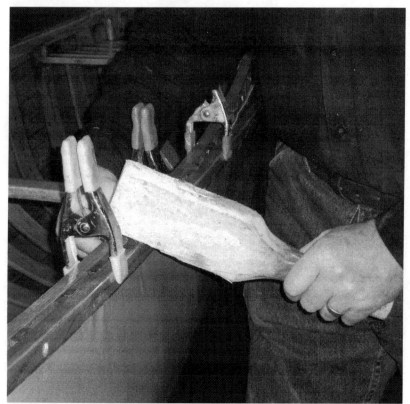

Be sure that the canvas is held smoothly against the hull as the outwale is clamped into place. Trim it where necessary to create a canvas free of bulges or creases along the sheer line.

Drill a pilot hole and counter-sink the screw so it will be secured below the surface of the outwale. A combination drill bit and countersink does this in one operation. Centre this hole on the outwale (top to bottom) and centre it with the rib as well. Throughout the rebuilding of the hull, do your best to keep the central area of the rib-top free of fasteners. When, as inevitably happens at least once in a canoe, you hit a fastener while making the pilot hole, simply angle the bit slightly to create a clear path for the screw.

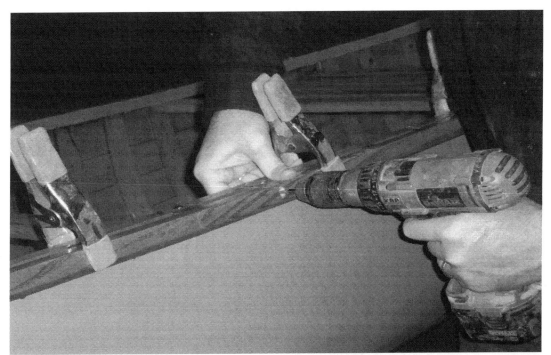

(Top) Drive the #8 bronze wood screw into the counter-sunk pilot hole.

(Bottom left) Use a sliding bevel and a permanent-ink marker to transfer the cut angle onto the outwale at the end of the canoe.

(Bottom right) Cut the end of the outwale with a Japanese cross-cut saw.

Attach the outwale to the canoe with #8 – 1½" (38 mm) flat head silicon-bronze screws. If you saved the original naval brass screws, use them to attach the outwales.

Once the outwale is attached, angle the cut ends of the outwales to give them a finished look. Use a sliding bevel to mark the angle and trim the new wood to length with a Japanese cross-cut saw.

Sand the cut-ends smooth and take the time to stain and varnish all of the newly exposed wood – including the screw holes. This is one of those little details that transforms the project from great to spectacular.

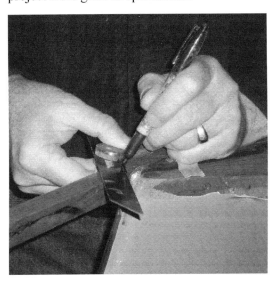

(Right) Use a steel punch to mark the centre of each seat spacer. This helps prevent the drill bit from wandering.

Seats

As it comes time to install the seats, many people use this as an opportunity to consider lowering them. Traditionally, most manufacturers set the seats between ¾" (19mm) and 1¼" (32mm) below the inwales. This allows the paddler to kneel in the canoe with their *gluteus maximus* (rear end) resting against the top edge of the seat. As knees get older, it becomes more difficult to kneel in the canoe. However, with the seat positioned just below the inwales and a person sitting on the seat, his or her centre of gravity is above the canoe. This results in a generally unstable arrangement. If the seats are hung about 2" (51mm), the paddler's centre of gravity is below the inwales. This creates a much more comfortable position for seated paddlers and still provides enough room under the seat to allow kneeling paddlers to get their feet into position. I am astounded at the difference in stability afforded by a relatively small drop in the seats.

Most canoe builders hung the seats from the inwales using 4" (10cm) carriage bolts and hardwood spacers. This system makes it fairly easy to lower the seats. Use 6" (15cm) carriage bolts and hardwood dowel for the new (longer) spacers.

(Below) Drill a hole down the centre of each seat spacer. If the spacer spins without wobbling, the drill bit is aligned straight down the centre axis.

The first step is to make the new spacers. The new bow seat spacers are 2¾" (70mm) long instead of the ¾" (19mm) originals. Since the inwales sweep up at the stern, the spacers must be two different lengths in order to keep the seat level. Therefore, the stern seat spacers are 2¾" (75mm) and 3¾" (95mm) long instead of the ¾" (19mm) and 1¾" (44mm) originals.

To accommodate the 3/16" (4.8mm) carriage bolt, a 13/64" (5.2mm) hole is drilled through the spacer from one end to the other. I have tried using a number of jigs for this procedure but, in the end, I now do it by hand – the same way they did it originally. Start by marking the centre of the dowel at each end with a steel punch. Then use a variable speed drill with a 13/64" bit to start the hole. The dimple created by the steel punch prevents the bit from wandering away from the centre of the dowel.

Begin drilling by lining it up as close to straight down the centre-line as you can determine by eye. Once the bit is established in the dowel, let it spin freely with the bit. If the dowel wobbles significantly as it spins, the bit is not aligned with the centre-line of the dowel. Adjust the alignment and drill a little further until the dowel spins smoothly without wobbling. Then, continue drilling until you are more than half way through. It helps to remove the bit and start again in order to clear waste wood from the hole as you drill.

Repeat this procedure from the other end of the dowel. If you have managed to centre the drill bit from both ends, you will end up with a hole straight through the dowel. Feed a carriage bolt through the spacer to ensure that the bolt is able to pass through easily. A little extra drilling may be required to give free passage to the bolt.

(Top) Stain the new seat spacers before applying shellac and varnish.

The spacers are now complete except for stain and finish. A small rack helps hold the spacers while they dry. My dowel rack is nothing more than eight 2½" (64mm) deck screws drilled through a scrap piece of 4/4 lumber.

To install the seats, use a ratcheting cargo strap to draw the sides of the canoe into the correct width. This is achieved when the bolts are aligned vertically and pass through the holes drilled at the ends of the seat frame. If your canoe has original inwales and seats, this is a very quick process. Sometimes the ends of the seat frames need to be trimmed slightly to allow them to fit in their new location in the canoe.

If the inwales or seat frames are new, holes will have to be drilled for the bolts. Again, use a steel punch to mark the position of the holes and prevent the drill bit from wandering. Set the carriage bolt into place with a wooden mallet. Secure the assembly with a bronze washer and nut. Tighten it with an adjustable wrench until the edge of the carriage bolt head has been drawn below the surface of the inwale. It is possible to over-tighten the bolts and snap them off, so be firm but not over-enthusiastic. If the bolt extends more than ¼" (6mm) past the nut, the excess can be trimmed with a hack saw to complete the job.

(Bottom) Use a couple of ratchet-straps to pull the canoe hull to the desired width prior to the installation of the seats.

(Top) Use a ratchet-strap to pull the hull in to the desired width for the thwart. Hold the thwart in place with two spring clamps on either side of the canoe.

Thwarts (Yoke)

If the thwarts and inwales are original, re-installing the thwarts is straightforward. They are attached directly under the inwales with 2" (5 cm) carriage bolts.

If the centre thwart is new or if you made a portage yoke, install the seats first. This will allow you to balance the canoe properly as you position the centre thwart (yoke). The balance point is somewhat subjective. Locate the thwart so the canoe balances comfortably for you.

Use a ratchet strap to draw the hull to the desired width. Then, hold the thwart (yoke) in place with two spring clamps on each side. Now, pick up the canoe and test the balance point. This is a matter of personal prefence, so work out a position that feels comfortable for you. Then attach the thwart (yoke) in much the same way as you attached the seats.

Decals

For some people, a wood-canvas canoe is not complete without the decals. I had one client put off having his canoe restored for years because he was afraid of losing the iconic Chestnut logo on the painted canvas. He kept the canvas on the canoe with miles of duck tape. He was surprised and delighted to learn that replacement decals are available.

Before applying "peel-and-stick" decals, wear clean vinyl gloves to avoid getting fingerprints and dust on the glued surface once the backing paper is removed.

Most deck decals are a traditional "slide" type where it is immersed in a jar of water for about two minutes so the decal can slide off the paper backing onto the canoe. Make sure the decal moves directly from the paper to the canoe deck.

Many Canadian canoe decals are available from the Canadian Canoe Museum while the Wooden Canoe Heritage Association carries decals for Old Town canoes.

(Below) Avoid getting fingerprints and dust on the "peel-and-stick" decal by wearing vinyl gloves.

Painter Rings

Painter rings are installed to provide a point of attachment for a length of rope used to secure the canoe to a dock. This rope – usually about 12' (3.65 meters) long – is called a "painter". The original painter ring on Chestnut and Peterborough canoes was a combination eye-bolt and ring located on the bow deck only. It was drilled through the deck and secured with a nut on the underside. I tend to use a bronze ring and a bronze eye-strap secured to the deck with two 1" #8 or #10 bronze wood screws. My personal choice is to attach painter rings to both bow and stern decks.

Decorative Designs

Decorative designs on canoes go back centuries to the native traditions of decorating birch bark canoes by scratching designs in the bark.

If you want a decorative design on your canoe, there are a couple of options. The easiest is to give your idea to a sign company and ask them to print it on vinyl. The "peel-and-stick" decal is applied in the usual manner.

The other option is to paint the design on the hull by hand. It usually involves the use of masking tape, ONE-SHOT® lettering enamel and an artist's brush. Having tried both methods, I prefer the use of vinyl decals. They are quick, clean and relatively inexpensive.

(Right) A bronze ring and eye strap are attached to each deck with two 1" #8 bronze wood screws

(Below) This 4-colour design was printed on vinyl by a sign company in a strip that was 3" (76 mm) high and 12' (3.65 meters) long.

(Left) "Hotrod Scallops" were painted on this canoe. Masking tape, lettering enamel and an artist's brush were used to do the job.

A Brand New Life

The Chestnut Prospector that was assessed in Chapter 2 was brought to my shop by a client who had two canoes in need of restoration. He had his 16' Chestnut Cruiser restored for his family and offered this 16' Prospector "up for adoption". Another client paid for the restoration, so it moved into a brand new home and a brand new life.

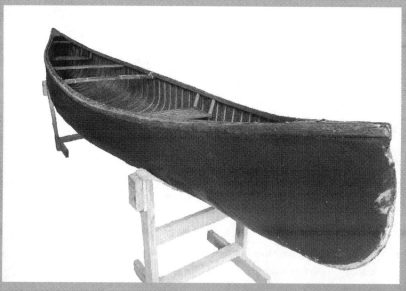

11
Care and Maintenance

Safe transport of your canoe starts with a high-quality roof rack. Attach the canoe at four points to create a secure ride.

Congratulations! Your canoe is fully restored and it looks so good, part of you just wants to stare at it all day. However, one of the best ways to care for your canoe is to take it out on the water on a regular basis. If it is tucked away safe and sound for years like a beautiful piece of antique furniture, it will dry out and become brittle. Your canoe needs to become an active member of the family again. Then it will thrive. Therefore, it needs to get to and from the water in one piece. It needs to be stored from one paddling season to the next without rotting away. It needs regular cosmetic maintenance and when something goes wrong, it needs some quick repairs in the field without having to start the restoration process all over again.

Safe Transport

Getting the canoe to the water safely can be one of the biggest challenges facing the canoeist. Here is the system I use to secure a canoe to the vehicle.

Roof Racks

Any secure roof rack on your vehicle will transport the canoe. Your fully restored canoe is worth several thousand dollars, so it only makes sense to invest a few hundred dollars in a top-quality roof rack. To avoid damage to the gunwales when they rub against the rack, place a piece of closed-cell foam between the canoe and the rack on each of the four contact points.

Ropes

Securing the canoe to the vehicle can be accomplished in any number of ways, yet to my mind, rope does the job well and serves double duty once the canoe is on the water. Use rope with a core made up of many straight fibers covered with a braided sheath.

This kind of rope has no 'memory' - that is, it can be knotted and untied without leaving bends or kinks in the rope. Climbing rope (9 mm) works very well but it sinks in water. Single braid polypropylene over a multi-fiber polypropylene core (3/8" MFP rope) has much the same construction as climbing rope and has the advantage of floating in water. Because it floats, MFP rope works very well as lining ropes (to guide an empty canoe through a rapid on a river from shore) and painters (12' - 3.7 meter ropes attached to the bow and stern decks of a canoe).

Anchor Loop

To tie the canoe to the roof rack, the end of the rope is anchored to the base of the rack by feeding the free end through a loop at the anchor end. The loop can be fashioned with many different knots, although I prefer a double figure-eight knot. This knot holds extremely well and forms an all-purpose anchor loop.

(Top left) Create an anchor loop with a double figure-eight knot. Multi-filament polypropylene (MFP) rope has no "memory" and it floats.

(Top right) By feeding the free end of the rope through the anchor loop around the base of the roof rack on one side, the rope cannot pop off in a violent gust of wind.

(Bottom) Protect the gunwales with a piece of closed-cell foam.

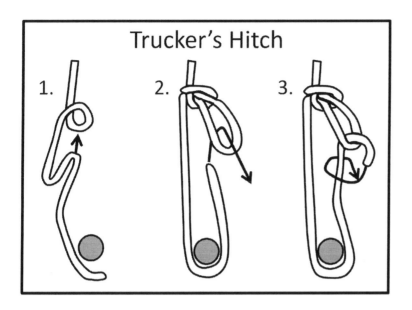

Trucker's Hitch

1.

2.

3.

(Above left and right) Secure the rope around the canoe with a "trucker's hitch".

Tying the Rope Tight

Toss the free end of the rope over the canoe and use a trucker's hitch to secure the canoe tightly to the rack. This is a compound knot involving a slip knot and a couple of half-hitches.

Begin by creating a slip knot with the free end. Loop the free-end around the canoe rack and pull it through the loop of the slip knot. Pull hard on the free-end to create lots of tension and hold the canoe tight to the rack. Pinch the rope where it passes through the slip knot loop and secure the free-end with a half-hitch and/or a slip-knot. Any extra rope in the free end is tucked away neatly with another half-hitch or slip-knot.

Securing the Ends of the Canoe

I use ¼" rope ratchets to secure both ends of the canoe to the vehicle. They are quick, easy to use and prevent the ends from twisting sideways in a strong wind.

The final touch is a flag attached to the rear carabiner. In some jurisdictions, it is required by law for anything that extends more than 12" (30cm) past the rear of the vehicle.

(Left) Secure both ends of the canoe on the roof rack with rope ratchets and a carabiner.

Canoe Storage Rack

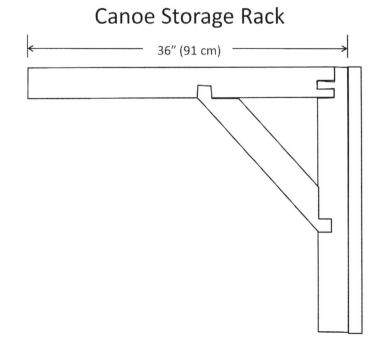

(Right) Canoe storage racks can be made of wood.

36" (91 cm)

Canoe Storage

Proper storage of your canoe is essential to ensure that it has a long, rot-free life. I'm sure there are as many ways to store a canoe as there are canoes. Let's look at a few.

As I have mentioned in Chapter 4, the fungi that cause wood rot can only grow in warm, damp environments. Therefore, it is best to store your canoe: 1) upside-down 2) well off the ground 3) in a cool, dry space away from the elements 4) with lots of air circulation.

Some examples of suitable spaces include: a) carport b) covered porch c) unheated garage d) lean-to shelter (against a building).

Once you have identified a viable location, the next step is to develop a storage method. I will describe three possible systems. From these, you ought to be able to come up with something that works for you.

A Basic Rack

Does your space have a solid wall on one side? Is there enough room away from the wall to allow access into the space? If so, simply build and install two racks about 7' (2 meters) apart. The racks can be made of wood or fabricated in steel. While a wooden rack requires bracing across the right-angle corner, good welds in a fabricated steel rack do not require extra bracing. Make sure the racks are secured well to the wall (with lag-bolts or through bolts and washers). Fit ABS pipe over the steel pipe to protect the canoe.

(Below) Good welds on steel tubing do not require extra bracing to support a canoe. Fit ABS pipe over the steel pipe to protect the canoes.

A Roller System

Is your storage space long and narrow? Is it awkward or impossible to access the space from the side? If so, feed the canoe into the space from one end. For this situation, install two support racks about 7' (2 meters) apart. Each support rack is a length of standard 1" (25 mm) steel pipe at least 40" (one meter) long threaded through a length of 1½" (38 mm) ABS pipe at least 36" (90 cm) long. Install each steel pipe securely at the desired height. The ABS pipe acts as a roller and makes it easy to store the canoe in and remove from a confined space.

A Hoist System

Is it possible or desirable to get your canoe up out of the way above everything else? If so, try using a system of ropes and pulleys to hoist your canoe up and away. Support the canoe with a length of rope wrapped around each end. Tie a permanent loop in both ends of each rope. Use a carabiner to clip the ends together to create a support loop for each end of the canoe. Then rig a length of ¼" (7 mm) braided rope (I use MFP rope) through a series of pulleys as illustrated below and install a cleat to secure the free-end of the rope.

(Left) A self-supporting canoe rack allows canoes to be loaded on and off from one end.

(Right) ABS pipe is threaded onto the steel pipe before fabricating the canoe rack. This creates a roller system for the rack.

(below) A hoist system can get the canoe up and out of the way while still making it easy to lower the canoe.

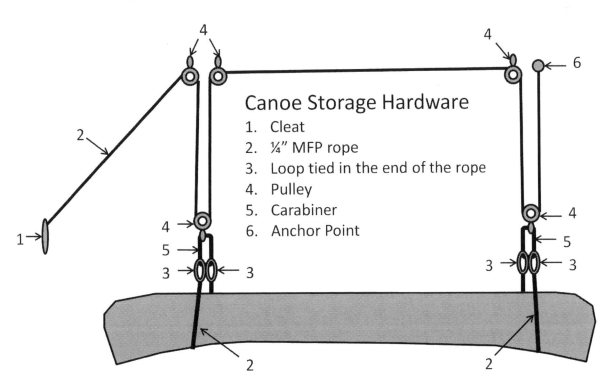

Canoe Storage Hardware

1. Cleat
2. ¼" MFP rope
3. Loop tied in the end of the rope
4. Pulley
5. Carabiner
6. Anchor Point

The case of the flying canoe

Fred had secured his newly restored Chestnut Pal to the rack on top of his truck. Unfortunately, he had not secured the ends. He was traveling 50 mph (80 km/hr) down the road when a strong cross-wind hit the vehicle causing the canoe to twist. This torque popped the straps free of the rack and Fred looked in the rearview mirror just in time to see his canoe hit the highway nose-first and skid along the asphalt.

When the canoe hit the pavement, all of the wood flexed, but did not break. Instead, all of the fasteners in the end broke or were torn loose.

I removed the stem-band, the starboard outwale and the broken fasteners from the deck. I clamped the end back together and secured the deck with new screws (pre-drilled with pilot holes). The canvas seam at the end had simply separated without tearing. It took only a few minutes to remove the old tacks and re-do the seam with new tacks. With the repairs completed, the outwale and stem-band were re-attached.

A light sanding followed by some paint touch-ups finished the repairs. The whole job took less than 90 minutes. Fred picked up his canoe the next day and went directly to the lake for a paddle. He now secures his canoe at four points instead of just two.

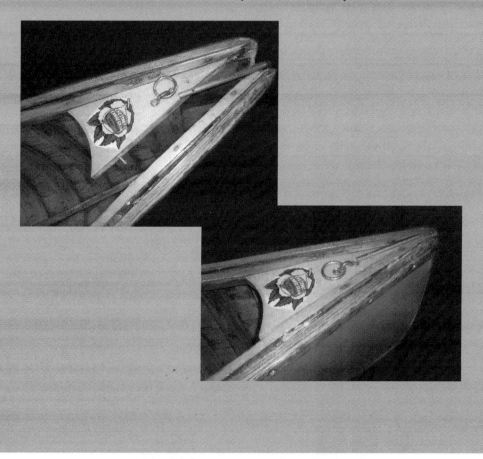

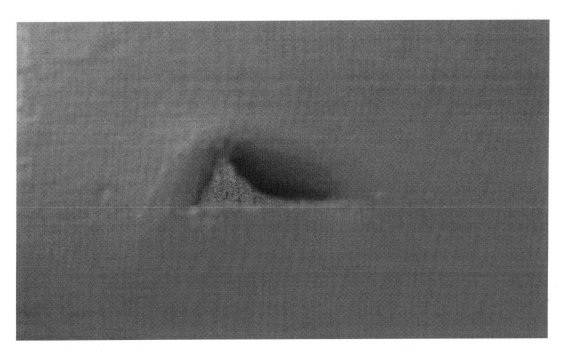

(Top) A tree branch poked a hole in the bottom of this canoe. Fortunately, no ribs were broken.

Patching a Hole

John was paddling on a large lake when a storm came up quickly. The canoe upset near a rocky shore in three-foot (one meter) waves, filled with water and was forced against the large branches of a deadfall. John couldn't get the canoe out of harm's way before a branch punched straight through the bottom of the canoe.

Fortunately, only one plank was damaged and there was no damage to the ribs. I put a new blade in my utility knife and "opened the patient". I cut longitudinally to about the centre of the rib on either side of the hole. Then, I cut transversely on both sides until I reached the edge of the plank both above and below the hole. The opening created enough room for tacks to secure both the new plank and the original one on both sides.

(Bottom) Cut flaps in the canvas to expose the broken plank.

(Top right) Remove the broken plank.

I used the utility knife to cut and remove the broken plank. At this point, it was a standard plank repair fitting between the two ribs. Once the new plank was cut to fit, it was secured with a total of 16 tacks. I drove the tacks from the outside while John held the clinching iron in place on the inside of the canoe.

I found a piece of scrap canvas (#10 – 14.5 ounce) in the shop and cut it to be just larger than the hole I created to make the plank repair. I poured a waterproof glue liberally over the canvas and spread it until the cloth was saturated on one side. Then, while John held the canvas away from the canoe, I used a thin scrap of hardwood to work the patch under the original canvas. I spread more Ambroid cement on the patch as well as the underside of the original canvas and then pressed the canvas down against the patch.

(Bottom right) Insert a canvas patch and glue it to the original canvas on its inside surface. Close the canvas opening with a number of canoe tacks. Then, fill the cut seams with two-part epoxy putty.

I "closed the patient" with 24 more tacks while John held the clinching iron on the inside of the canoe. I then filled the rough edged of the cuts with two-part epoxy putty to complete the repair job. A little sanding followed by some touch-up paint on the outside as well as some stain, shellac and varnish on the new wood on the interior made the repair very difficult to see.

(Below) Secure the new plank with a number of canoe tacks.

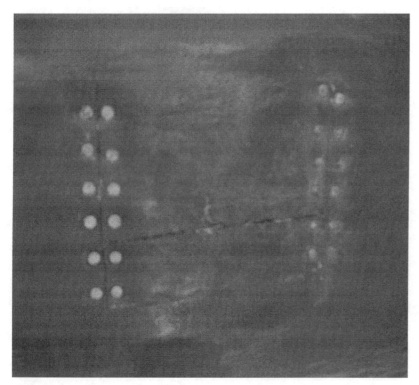

Touch-Ups

The long term health of your canoe is maintained with regular use as long as you resist the temptation to run it up on the beach or take it through a rock garden in a river at low water. That said, the paint on the canvas will get a few scuffs and scrapes over the years and varnish on the exposed wood (especially on the outwales) will wear off in a few spots. Every couple of years, go over the canoe and sand the areas that need a little attention (use 120-grit sandpaper). Apply paint and varnish (thinned 12% with paint thinner) to the affected areas and let them dry for 48 hours. As with many things, a little timely effort now saves a lot of work later on.

In case of emergency

As I was completing the restoration of an 18′ Chestnut Prospector Vee-Stern canoe for a client, he asked me to create a wood-canvas canoe field repair kit. He lives in Whitehorse and plans to use the canoe on hunting trips in the Yukon. A few basic supplies along with a hammer, a screwdriver and the obligatory roll of duct tape are all you need to hold your canoe together until you get out of the bush and back to civilization.

The kit fits into a small food container (900 ml or 30.4 fluid ounces) and consists of the following items:

• a piece of #10 (14.5 ounce) canvas 12″x12″ (30 cm x 30 cm)
• 10′ (3 meters) of 3/16″ rawhide lacing (babiche)
• a tube of waterproof glue
• 30 - 3/4″ (19 mm) brass canoe tacks
• 20 - 3/4″ (19 mm) silicon bronze 14-gauge ring nails
• 12 - 1″ #8 silicon bronze flat-head square-drive wood screws
• a small container of alkyd enamel paint

You could also pack a clinching iron (auto-body dolly) but I don't see the need when a river rock will do the trick just as well. Most of the supplies are self-explanatory except for the babiche. It is very useful for lashing a broken thwart back together or holding a make-shift thwart (tree branch) in place. Soak the babiche for a few hours, do your lashing and wait a few hours for it to dry. The babiche will tighten and hold anything without fail.

12
Restorers' Guide

The 16' Pleasure canoe built by the Chestnut Canoe Company (called the Pal) is perhaps the best general-purpose canoe ever built. Many people mistake it for the legendary Chestnut Prospector.

W hile restoring your wood-canvas canoe, you will probably have a few questions. The first and most common question is, "Who made my canoe?" The next question has to do with the dimensions of various components in your canoe. Most of the time, you can take the dimensions from the existing piece. However, there are times when the original component no longer exists. So, in this chapter I present a "Restorer's Guide" to wood-canvas canoes that covers some typical styles of wood-canvas canoe. I will start with a look at some of the canoes produced by the Chestnut Canoe Company. I will then present specific dimensions for five canoes that are representative of many canoes you may encounter.

A Chestnut Canoe Primer

In Canada, the canoes from the Chestnut Canoe Company set the standard by which all others are measured. Now, many decades after the company went out of business, they are still held up as classic canoe icons. So, how can you identify a canoe as a Chestnut and what makes a Prospector a Prospector?

The Chestnut Canoe Company

William and Henry Chestnut started building wood-canvas canoes in 1897. They bought a canoe in Maine (probably a Gerrish canoe) and made exact copies of it which they sold out of their father's furniture business in Fredericton, New Brunswick. They obtained the Canadian patent for wood-canvas canoe construction in 1905 which many people regard as the birth of the company. However, the 1972 Chestnut Canoe Company catalogue proudly celebrated 75 years in business. It seems the company viewed its birth as 1897. Be that as it may, the company grew into the largest canoe manufacturer in Canada. At its height, they produced in excess of 3,000 canoes per year. In 1923, Chestnut Canoe Company and Peterborough Canoe Company amalgamated under an umbrella group called Canadian Watercraft Limited (followed later by the Canadian Canoe Company). As a result, the wood-canvas canoes for all three companies had very similar lines. Some suspect the canvas-covered canoes for all three companies were built at the Chestnut factory in Fredericton. The Peterborough Canoe Company ceased operations in 1961 while the Chestnut Canoe Company closed its doors in 1978.

Chestnut produced over 50 different canoes to suit a variety of needs. However, I will focus on five Chestnut canoes: Ogilvy, Cruiser, Bobs Special, Pleasure and Prospector.

The Chestnut Ogilvy

Fishing guides on the salmon rivers of New Brunswick needed river canoes they could stand up in all day long. They were often poling the canoe upstream through shallow rapids in order to offer the prime fishing spots to their clients. The canoe had to be stable and tough with a shallow draft. The Ogilvy brothers were fishing guides in New Brunswick and helped design the Ogilvy model for the Chestnut Canoe Company. They came in six lengths that ranged from 16' to 26'. Though never as popular as others, they are real, honest, working canoes.

The ribs in Ogilvy canoes are 3" wide, 3/8" thick and have only ½" space between them. This creates what amounts to a double-planked hull. The rugged nature of the Ogilvy comes with a price in terms of weight. The 16' has an average weight of 84 pounds and a carrying capacity of 850 pounds. It has a flat-bottomed hull, straight sides, full entry lines and modest rocker in the ends. This makes for a canoe that is slow and steady – exactly what is needed when working shallow, rapid rivers with few, if any portages.

(Right) The Chestnut Ogilvy has a wide, flat bottom and a strong, solid floor. This allowed professional fishing guides to stand up in the canoe all day long.

(Left) The Chestnut Cruiser has a narrow, semi-arched hull and fine entry lines to create a fast, maneuverable river canoe. Recommended for the "expert" canoeist.

The Chestnut Cruiser

The Chestnut Cruiser was one of the first canoes they developed. It was influenced very heavily by (if not copied directly from) Gerrish, White and Morris canoes built in Maine in the late 1890's. The lines are sleek, narrow and graceful – designed to handle rivers with speed and efficiency. This narrow canoe has an arched bottom, fine-entry lines and generous rocker at the ends. Therefore, it is not for the novice paddler. However, in the hands of someone who knows what to do, this canoe is a dream to paddle.

(Bottom) The Chestnut Cruiser was built for speed -- long and narrow with a rounded bottom.

(Top) The Bobs Special is both light-weight (58 pounds or 26 kilograms) and stable. It was a very popular general-purpose canoe.

The Chestnut Bobs Special

The Bobs Special was one of two lightweight pleasure canoes built by the Chestnut Canoe Company. Before I talk about the canoe, I'd like to clarify the name. In the early 1900's, Chestnut received orders from across the country by telegraph. Rather than go through the time and expense of describing the length, model and options of each canoe in a long, costly telegram, the Chestnut company assigned short names to each canoe model. These "telegraph codes" began as a convenient and cost-effective way to describe the canoes in a purchase order. However, they quickly became model names used by the general public.

According to Roger MacGregor in his book *When the Chestnut was in Flower*, Henry and William were real history buffs. The telegraph code for the 15' 50-lb. Special was BOBS and made reference to Lord Roberts, a major figure during the Boer War in South Africa. Over the years, as this wide, light-weight canoe became more difficult to keep under the weight limit of 50 lbs (the average weight was 58 pounds), they changed the name. I have seen a variety of Chestnut catalogues call it "Bob's Special", "Bob Special" and "Bobs Special". So, feel free to take your pick.

(Left) The Bobs Special paddles very easily which is surprising for a wide, stable canoe.

Many outdoor enthusiasts look for a light-weight, stable canoe that would allow them to enjoy fly fishing or just a quiet paddle on the lake. With a 37" beam and 12½" depth at the centre, the Bobs Special is very stable — ideal for those who find a regular canoe too 'tippy'. At the same time, it is surprisingly quick and maneuverable in the water. This is due to the shallow-arch bottom combined with moderate rocker and fine entry lines in the ends. The ribs are 2-3/8" wide and ¼" thick with 1½" spaces between them.

The Chestnut Pleasure Canoes

Bill Mason (1929 - 1988) was a Canadian naturalist, author, artist, filmmaker, and conservationist who played a major role in revitalizing the popularity of canoes and canoeing in Canada during the 1970's through a series of books and films. It is no accident that he used a 16' Chestnut Pal in most of his films. It is stable, yet quick; steady, yet agile. With a 36" beam, 12¾" depth at the centre, weight of 72 pounds and a carrying capacity of 700 pounds, the Pal is as close to being a perfect recreational canoe as you ever hope to get. It is one of the Chestnut Pleasure canoe models which also include 14' and 15' lengths. Until 1958, the 16' Pleasure canoe had a 34" beam. Then, the mould was widened. The economy version of the 16' Pleasure canoe had been called the Pal for several years (from about 1954). The Pleasure canoes came in both narrow and wide versions until about 1960 when the wider versions were adopted exclusively. Over the years, the ribs of the pleasure canoes came in two different sizes – either 1½" wide or 2-3/8" wide.

The bottom is a shallow-arch hull with tumblehome extending through the entire length of the canoe. The fine entry lines and moderate rocker make it very easy to paddle. In his film, *Path of the Paddle: Solo Whitewater*, Bill Mason demonstrated very well that the Pal is not designed for Class 3 rapids. But, that didn't stop him from trying. The Pal is a great general-purpose canoe and has been the canoe of choice for many generations of canoeists – even if many of them call it a Chestnut Prospector.

(Above) The wide, semi-arched bottom makes the Chestnut Pal easy to paddle without being "tippy".

(Left) The Chestnut Pal has a perfect combination of design features to make it both stable and agile.

(Right) The arched bottom of the Prospector makes it quick in the water and some people complain that it feels "tippy" when they first get into the canoe. The hull flares near the ends to turn waves away.

The Chestnut Prospector

This is the real deal – often copied, never matched. A quick search on the internet produces at least ten modern canoe companies with a "Prospector" in their catalogues. However, the Chestnut Canoe Company found the winning combination. With high sides, substantial arch in the bottom and lots of rocker in the full ends, it is designed to transport heavy loads quickly through rapid rivers and large, challenging lakes. It is essentially a deeper, wider Cruiser and is still regarded as the ultimate wilderness tripping canoe.

The Chestnut Prospector is a fun canoe to paddle solo. Kneeling in the centre, sitting on your heels with your body tucked into the chine on one side, the hull rolls to that side and settles into a stable position with the gunwales just a couple of inches above the water. In this position, the ends rise high in the air and create a short play-boat to spin and dance on the water. However, it really comes into its own when loaded for an extended trip. Although there is good tumblehome at the centre, the hull flares about 4' from the ends in order to throw water away from the canoe while hitting big waves in rapid rivers. It was built as a working canoe with solid hardwood slat seats instead of the hand-woven cane seats found in most other Chestnut canoes.

(Bottom) The Chestnut Prospector is the ultimate wildness tripping canoe.

Chestnut Canoe Colours

Ryan grew up in the family canoe. He and his father paddled their Bobs Special all over the country. When he walked into my shop to pick up the restored canoe, he exclaimed, "It's the same colour!"

Over the years, various clients have given me cans of the original Chestnut paint that they had saved for 40 years. I live in a small town in the southern interior of British Columbia. Our local hardware store is part of a nation-wide chain that has a computerized colour-matching system in their paint department. They colour-matched each of the three Chestnut canoe colours (these colours are the same for Peterborough canoes as well). Here are the paint codes for those iconic colours.

Note: The mix for Chestnut Red is in a clear base which does not cover well. It is translucent. To have the colour work well, use a factory mixed red for the first two coats. Then, apply two coats of Chestnut Red with a bristle brush and a final coat with a foam brush. The resulting five coats produces a finish that is even and consistent.

Chestnut Red   (Pleasure and Lightweight models)
Exterior/Alkyd/Rust Coat
Clear Base

Daylight	Colour	Ounces	Shots	Half Shots
64-03	C	0	43	1
Gallon	G	0	0	1
	R	8	25	1

Chestnut Green - Dark Green   (Pleasure and Lightweight models)
Exterior/Alkyd/Rust Coat
Clear Base

Daylight	Colour	Ounces	Shots	Half Shots
64-03	C	2	40	1
Gallon	D	2	22	1
	G	0	14	1
	Z	3	37	1

Chestnut Grey - Light Green   (Cruiser, Prospector and Ogilvy models)
Exterior/Alkyd/Rust Coat
Medium Base

Daylight	Colour	Ounces	Shots	Half Shots
Medium (04)	B	2	22	0
Gallon	C	5	4	1
	G	1	14	1
	Z	0	38	1

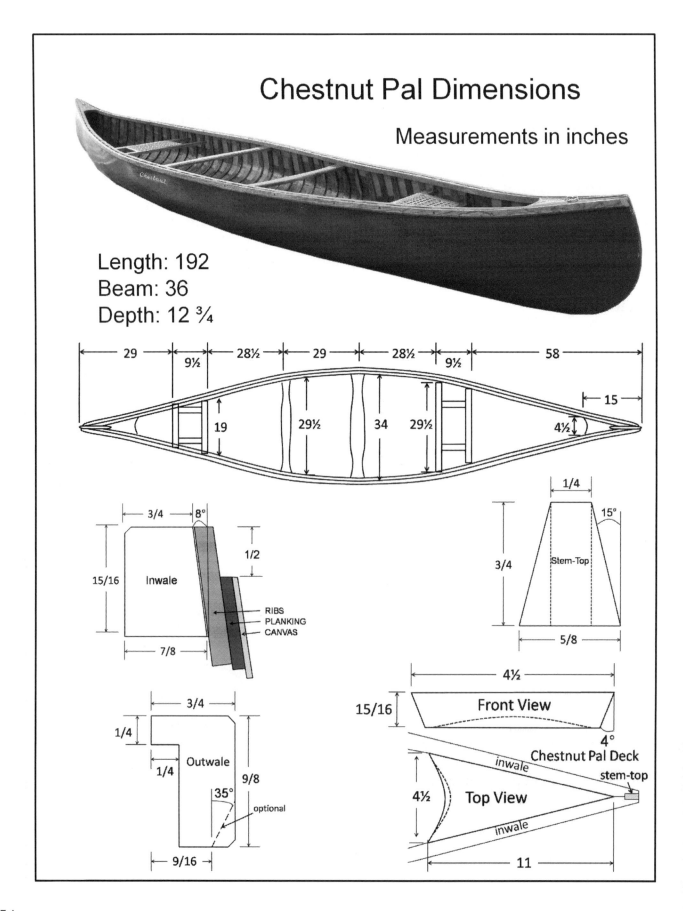

Chestnut Pal Dimensions

Measurements in inches

Length: 192
Beam: 36
Depth: 12 ¾

29   9½   28½   29   28½   9½   58

19   29½   34   29½   4½   15

3/4   8°
1/2
15/16   Inwale
7/8

RIBS
PLANKING
CANVAS

1/4
3/4
Stem-Top
5/8

3/4
1/4   3/4
Outwale
1/4   9/8
35°   optional
9/16

4½
15/16   Front View
4°
Chestnut Pal Deck
stem-top
inwale
4½   Top View
inwale
11

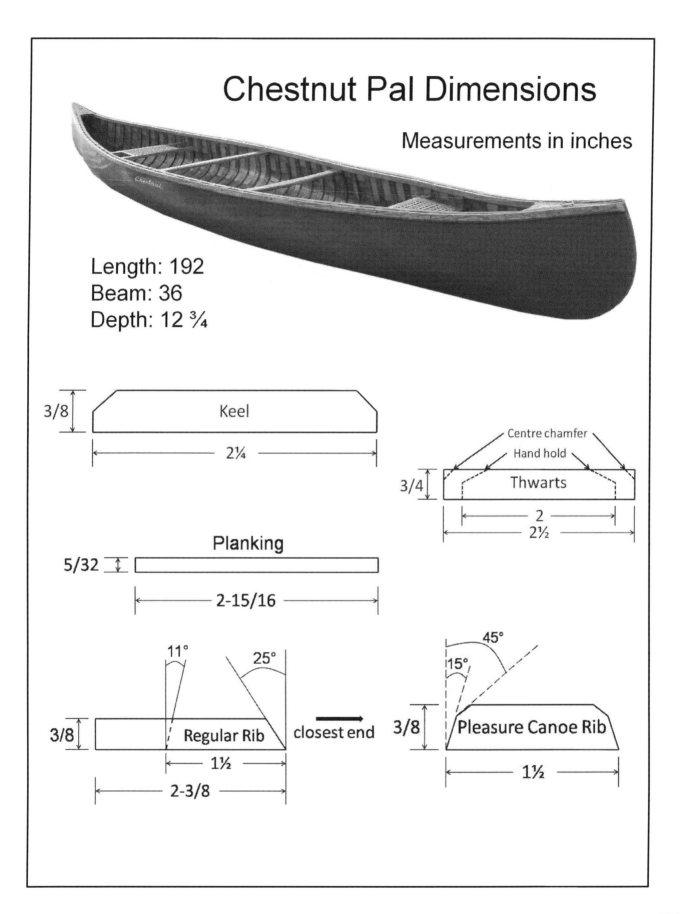

Chestnut Pal Dimensions

Measurements in inches

Length: 192
Beam: 36
Depth: 12 ¾

Keel

3/8

2¼

Centre chamfer

Hand hold

Thwarts

3/4

2

2½

Planking

5/32

2-15/16

11°   25°

3/8   Regular Rib   closest end

1½

2-3/8

45°

15°

3/8   Pleasure Canoe Rib

1½

Chestnut Bobs Special Dimensions

Measurements in inches

Length: 180
Beam: 37
Depth: 12 ¾

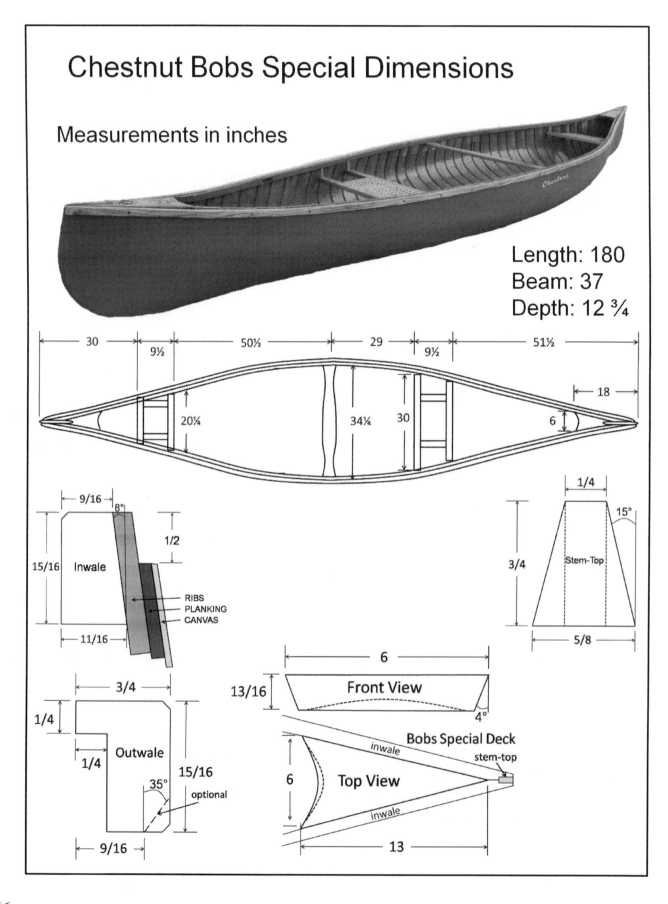

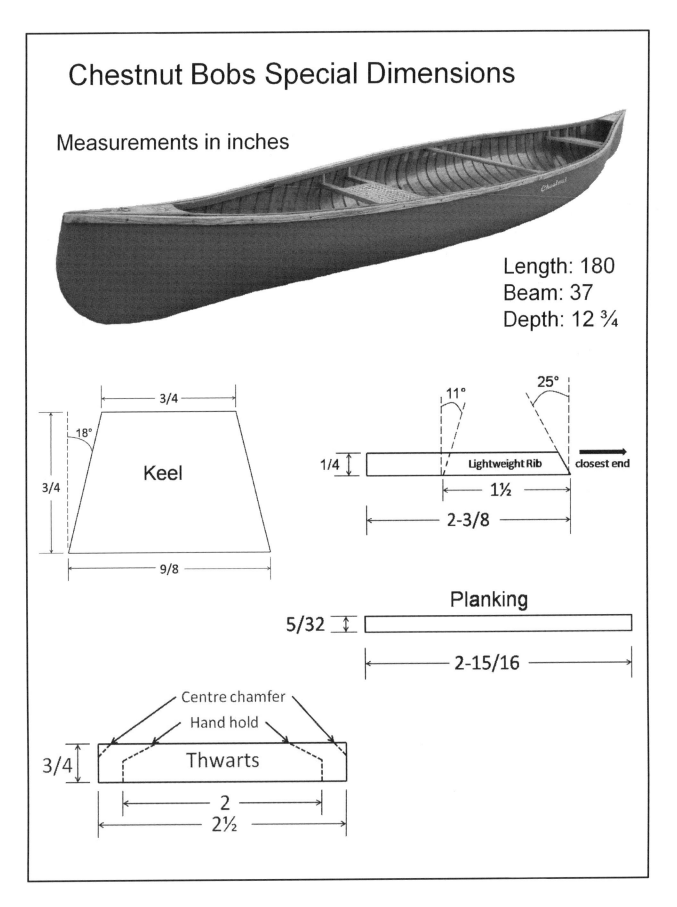

Chestnut Bobs Special Dimensions

Measurements in inches

Length: 180
Beam: 37
Depth: 12 ¾

Keel

3/4

18°

3/4

9/8

11°   25°

1/4   Lightweight Rib   closest end

1½

2-3/8

Planking

5/32

2-15/16

Centre chamfer

Hand hold

Thwarts

3/4

2

2½

Table of Specifications for Selected Chestnut Canoes
(from Chestnut Canoe Company catalogue 1972)

TYPE	STYLE	MODEL	Length Overall	Beam midship	Depth midship	Rib Thickness	Rib Spacing	No. of Thwarts	Weight	Carrying Capacity	Seat Type&No.	Keel
Pleasure Canoes	Economy	Fox	14'	32"	11.75"	0.375"x 1.50"	1.50"	1	60 lbs	500 lbs	2 cane	shoe
		Doe	15'	34"	12.50"			1	68 lbs	600 lbs		
		Deer	16'	36"	12.75"			2	72 lbs	700 lbs		
	Standard	Playmate	14'	32"	11.75"	0.375"x 2.375"	2.00"	1	60 lbs	500 lbs	2 cane	shoe
		Chum	15'	34"	12.50"			1	68 lbs	600 lbs		
		Pal	16'	36"	12.75"			2	72 lbs	700 lbs		
Lightweight Canoes		Bob Special	15'	37"	12.75"	0.25"x 2.375"	1.50"	1	58 lbs	700 lbs	2 cane	taper
		Featherweight	11'	34"	12.50"			2	40 lbs	350 lbs	1 cane	shoe
Cruiser Canoes	Standard	Kruger	16'	33"	13.25"	0.375"x 2.375"	2.00"	4	70 lbs	600 lbs	2 cane	none
		Cronje	17'	34"	13.00"			5	75 lbs	650 lbs		
		Leader	18'	35"	13.25"			5	79 lbs	700 lbs		
	Guides Special	Boone	16'	33"	13.25"		0.50"	4	75 lbs	600 lbs	2 cane	none
		Crocket	17'	34"	13.00"			5	80 lbs	650 lbs		
		Moses	18'	35"	13.25"			5	85 lbs	700 lbs		
Prospector Canoes	Pointed Stern	Fire	14'	33"	13.75"	0.375"x 2.375"	2.00"	1	63 lbs	600 lbs	2 slat	none
		Ranger	15'	35"	13.50"			1	70 lbs	650 lbs		
		Fort	16'	36"	14.50"			2	76 lbs	850 lbs		
		Garry	17'	37"	14.50"			3	82 lbs	950 lbs		
		Voyageur	18'	38"	15.00"			3	88 lbs	1100 lbs		
	Vee Stern	Elk	14'	33"	13.75"		2.00"	3	72 lbs	600 lbs	2 slat	taper
		Bear	15'	35"	13.50"			3	80 lbs	650 lbs		
		Fawn	16'	36"	14.50"			3	82 lbs	850 lbs		
		Marsh	17'	37"	14.50"			4	97 lbs	950 lbs		
		Birch	18'	38"	15.00"			4	110 lbs	1100 lbs		
Ogilvy Canoes	Pointed Stern	Henry	16'	36"	13.50"	0.375"x 2.375"	0.50"	2	84 lbs	850 lbs	2 cane	none
		Dave	18'	36"	13.50"			4	95 lbs	1000 lbs		none
		Jock	20'	37"	14.00"			4	108 lbs	1300 lbs		none
		Alex	22'	38"	15.00"			4	125 lbs	1500 lbs		none
		Joe	24'	40"	14.00"			5	150 lbs	1800 lbs		taper
		Chief	26'	41"	14.00"			5	175 lbs	2000 lbs		taper
	Vee Stern	Parr	16'	36"	13.50"		0.50"	3	92 lbs	850 lbs	2 cane	taper
		Grilse	18'	36"	13.50"			5	103 lbs	1000 lbs		
		Pool	20'	37"	14.00"			5	118 lbs	1300 lbs		
		Trout	22'	38"	15.00"			5	185 lbs	1500 lbs		
		Salar	24'	40"	14.00"			6	240 lbs	1800 lbs		
		Salmo	26'	41"	14.00"			6	275 lbs	2000 lbs		

The 15'-6" "Huron" Canoe

Huron village – also known as Lorette or Loretteville – became Wendake in 1986 and is now a suburb north-west of Québec City. Canoes and canoe building have been part of the town's heritage since it was established in 1697. Builders such as Bastien Brothers, Sioui, Gagnon Brothers, Groslouis, Faber, Picard, Big Chief and Yaho made canoes under their own names. Thousands of canoes were also produced generically and sold through the Sears catalogue from the 1920's through to the early 1970's.

When I was a boy in the early 1960's, people referred to "Huron" canoes as "The Poor Man's Chestnut". At the time, a "Huron" could be purchased for about half the price of a similar canoe made by the Chestnut Canoe Company. I have had many people contact me about restoring their canoe insisting it is a Chestnut canoe. Often, they seem disappointed to learn they own a "Huron". However, to my mind, "Hurons" are amongst the finest canoes ever built. Their rough and ready appearance has grown on me. You can say they are the Volkswagen Beetle of canoes, only this Volkswagen performs like a Ferrari. The lines of "Huron" canoes work beautifully on the water.

I tip my hat to all of the First Nations builders in Wendake. They knew what they were doing. The lines of these canoes can be traced back to the birch-bark canoes of the area. They hold a classic elegance that overrides any cosmetic shortcomings.

Gunwales

"Huron" canoe gunwales consist of three components. The inwale is a rough piece of spruce. For a 15'-6" canoe, the inwales were 14' long while the 13'-6" canoe had 12' inwales. The last 9" or so of the inwales at each end are tapered down to 5/8" wide to fit into the decks. All of the transverse components are attached to the inwales with 10-24 (3/16") steel machine bolts. All of these attachments are rough looking, so they were covered up with a spruce gunwale-cap. The outwales were originally made of spruce as well. I always replace the outwales with hardwood – usually ash or oak. If I am

replacing the inwales I use hardwood as well (again ash or oak) and cut them to ¾" wide to reduce the weight of the component while maintaining the overall strength. Consequently, the gunwale cap is also ¾" wide.

Decks

The decks in a "Huron" canoe were built very roughly. They used a slab of birch or maple that varied in thickness from ¾" to more than 1". The stem-top sits flush with the nose of the deck and is held in place with a steel common nail. By the time you start restoring your canoe, the decks are usually rotted along with the stem-top. What is left of the common nail is often sticking out of the rotted nose of the deck. I replace the deck with maple and take the time to polish it in sandpaper progressive steps to 600-grit. I attach the rebuilt stem-top to the nose of the deck with a 1½" #8 bronze wood screws. The base of the deck sits 18" from the end.

Planking

Many people worry about the gaps between the planks in a "Huron" canoe. The original canoe was constructed with green wood that subsequently shrunk to create spaces between the planks that can be as much as ¼" wide. ***Do not try to fill the spaces with anything.*** It will only result in a mess that some other restorer will have to deal with the next time the canoe is restored. The gaps you see are one of the defining features that make "Huron" canoes what they are. The spaces do not compromise the strength of the hull, so you can maintain the authenticity of your "Huron" by matching the width of the original planks even though you are deliberately leaving gaps between the planks.

The planking is attached to the ribs with two tacks to each rib throughout much of the hull. Most other canoe companies used three or even four tacks on planks of the same width. Consequently, Huron canoes tend to flex more than other canoes. By the time you get to your "Huron" canoe, many of the tacks have probably worked loose. I spend a lot of time re-clinching and replacing tacks in these canoes. I also add about 500 tacks to the hull to give it greater strength and durability.

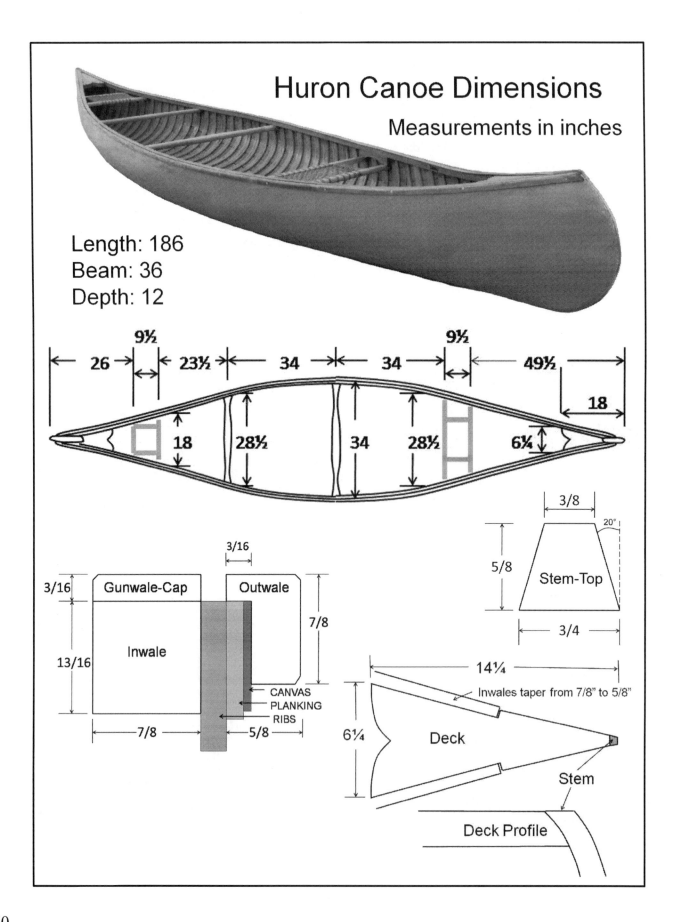

Huron Canoe Dimensions

Measurements in inches

Length: 186
Beam: 36
Depth: 12

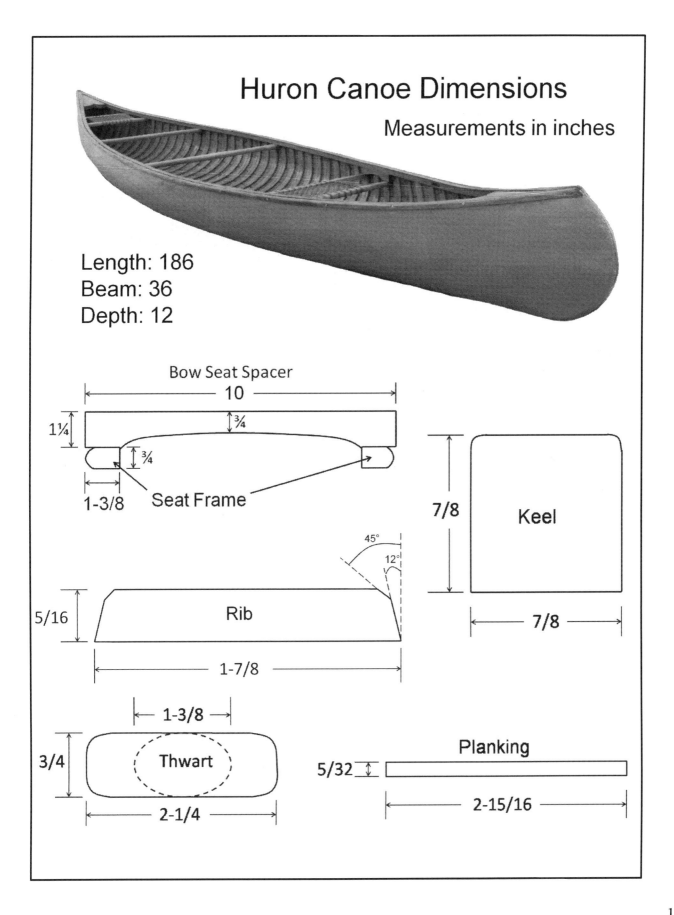

Huron Canoe Dimensions

Measurements in inches

Length: 186
Beam: 36
Depth: 12

Bow Seat Spacer
10
1¼
¾
¾
1-3/8
Seat Frame

Keel
7/8
7/8

45°
12°
Rib
5/16
1-7/8

1-3/8
Thwart
3/4
2-1/4

Planking
5/32
2-15/16

(Top) Tremblay canoes are stable, rugged and nicely finished with mahogany trim.

A Tremblay Canoe

Of the lesser known canoe manufacturers in Canada, Tremblay Canoes Limited (Les Canots Tremblay Limitée) from St. Félicien, Québec stood out from the crowd. They were well constructed with mahogany trim and their sweet lines made for a lovely paddling canoe.

The specifications I present here are for the standard line of canoes produced by Tremblay known collectively as the Chibougamau canoes. There were six canoes in the Chibougamau line ranging in length from 14' to 20'.

Hand Thwarts

Hand thwarts are carrying handles on both ends of the canoe. They are positioned about 7" back from each deck and are made from birch or maple with nicely rounded edges.

Portage Yoke

If present in your canoe, you will appreciate the lovely shape of this yoke. It is made of ash 5¾" wide tapering to 2¼" at the ends. Like most designs that are pleasing to the eye, it is also very comfortable to use.

(Below) The Tremblay portage yoke was both functional and attractive.

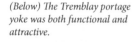

(Bottom) The Tremblay Canoes decal.

Seats

The seat frames are made of ¾" birch or maple that is 1-1/8" wide. Both seats are attached to mahogany braces on either side of the canoe with 1½" #8 bronze wood screws. The seats are approximately 2" below the inwale. The body of the seat is laced rawhide done the same way snowshoes were laced.

(Top) The seats in Tremblay canoes are laced with rawhide in exactly the same fashion as snowshoes.

(Bottom) The convex deck along with the simple maple hand thwarts and elegant rawhide seats identify this as a Tremblay canoe.

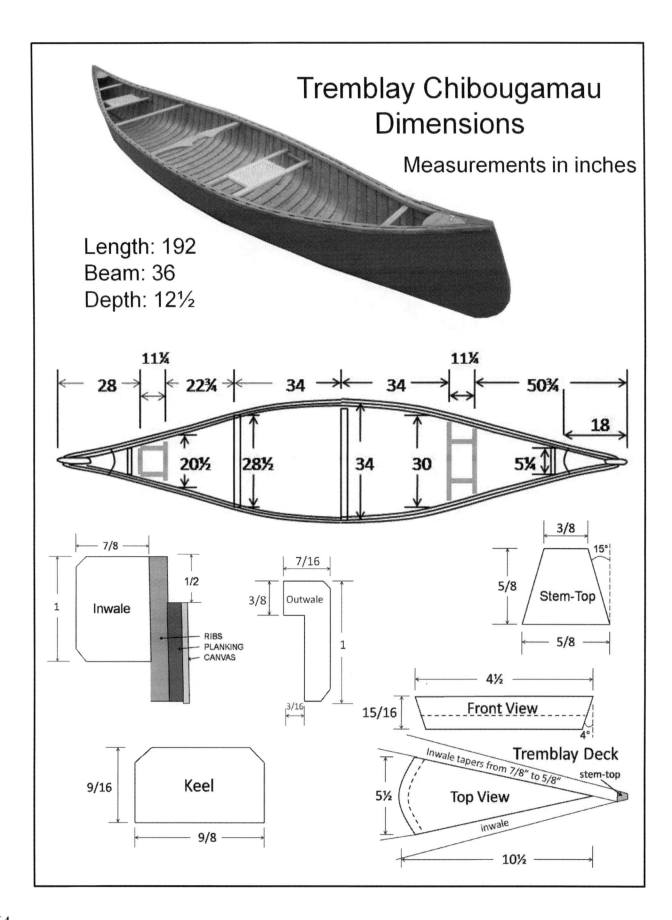

Tremblay Chibougamau Dimensions

Measurements in inches

Length: 192
Beam: 36
Depth: 12½

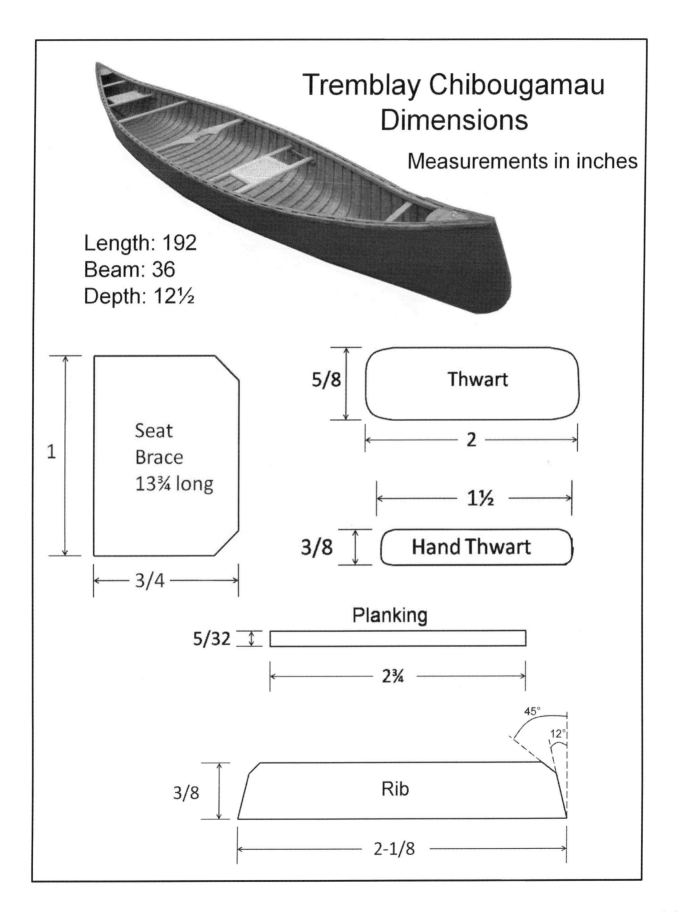

Tremblay Chibougamau Dimensions

Measurements in inches

Length: 192
Beam: 36
Depth: 12½

Seat
Brace
13¾ long

1

3/4

5/8

Thwart

2

1½

3/8

Hand Thwart

Planking

5/32

2¾

45°

12°

3/8

Rib

2-1/8

A "Maine Guide" Canoe

The "Maine Guide" canoe was designed specifically to navigate the shallow, rapid salmon rivers in northern Maine. The lines were taken directly from the Malecite and Passamaquoddy birch-bark canoes of the area. Among the builders that produced them are names such as E.H. Gerrish, E.M. White, B.N. Morris and, of course, Old Town canoes. In fact, Old Town alone has produced more than 200,000 wood-canvas canoes since they began in 1901.

The "Maine Guide" canoe is designed to be stable. The fishing guide would stand up in the canoe and pole upstream in order to get his client to the best salmon fishing spots on the river. Typically, some of the features of this canoe include: 1) a wide, flat bottom 2) substantial tumblehome along the full length 3) half ribs between the main ribs 4) no centre thwart in some models 5) a strongly curved stem profile 6) a graceful taper at the ends of the inwales 7) Philippine mahogany (luan) used for all of the structural components.

Maine Guide canoes are trimmed in mahogany with beautiful finish details. This canoe was built by Bill Greenwood in British Columbia, Canada and is typical of the Maine Guide canoe style.

I would love to be able to present dimensions for these specific component parts. Unfortunately, I have yet to see an E.H. White or B.N. Morris canoe here in British Columbia. However, I have restored many Greenwood canoes.

Bill Greenwood travelled from Vancouver, BC to Old Town, Maine in 1934. He wanted to build canoes, so he hung around the Old Town Canoe Company factory until they figured out what he was doing and kicked "the spy" out. He returned to BC and opened his Greenwood Watercraft Company. He had several locations before he established a large facility on Mitchell Island in Richmond, BC where he and a couple of workers produced about 300 canoes a year through the 1960's until a fire destroyed the factory in 1970. He rebuilt the business on a smaller scale and sold it in 1975. His workmanship was outstanding and Greenwood canoes have a loyal following that persists to this day.

Greenwood canoes can be considered typical of Maine Guide canoes since they have all of the features usually found in this style of canoe.

Maine Guide Canoe Seat Frame

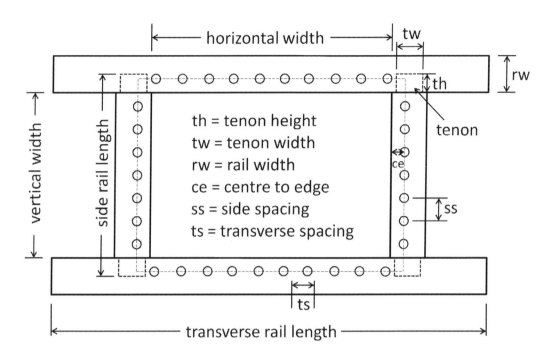

th = tenon height
tw = tenon width
rw = rail width
ce = centre to edge
ss = side spacing
ts = transverse spacing

Component	Position	Imperial
Transverse rail (length)	Bow	34.00"
	Stern	24.00"
Side rail (length)	Bow	8.50"
	Stern	9.50"
Horizontal width (internal)	Bow	11.25"
	Stern	8.75"
Vertical width (internal)	Bow	7.00"
	Stern	8.00"
Seat frame stock	Width	1-3/4"
	Thickness	7/8"
Tenon	Width	1-3/8"
	Height	3/4"
	Thickness	3/8"
Holes	Diameter	3/16"
Centre of hole to	inside edge	1/2"
Hole Spacing	Transverse	7/8"
	Side	1.00"
Transverse Holes (number)	Bow	13
	Stern	10
Side Holes (number)	Bow	7
	Stern	8

(Above) Hand-woven cane seats in the Maine Guide canoe style have Philippine mahogany (luan) frames, square seat spacers and no couching in the cane weaving pattern.

167

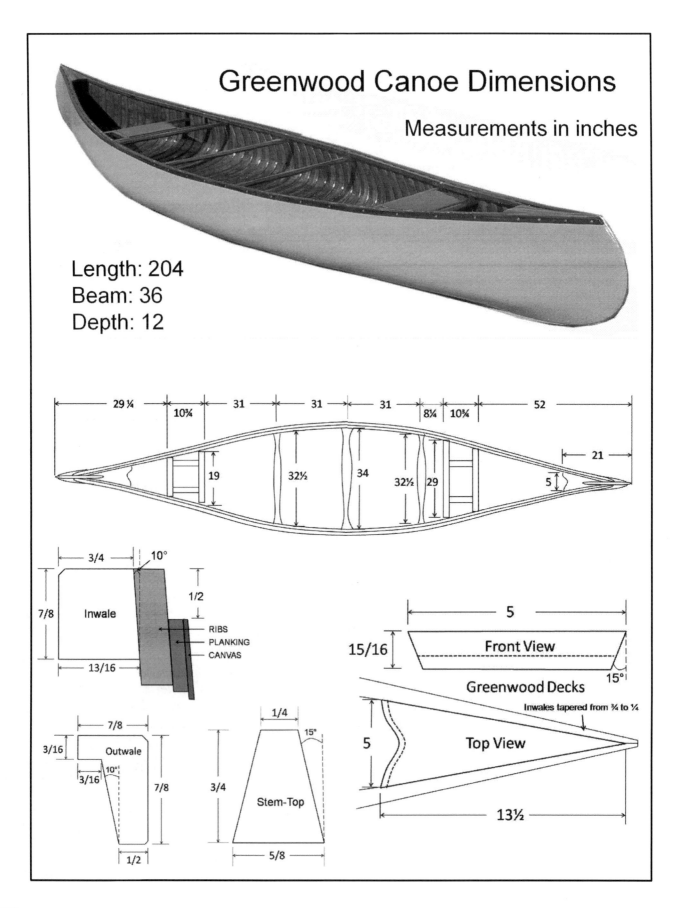

Greenwood Canoe Dimensions

Measurements in inches

Length: 204
Beam: 36
Depth: 12

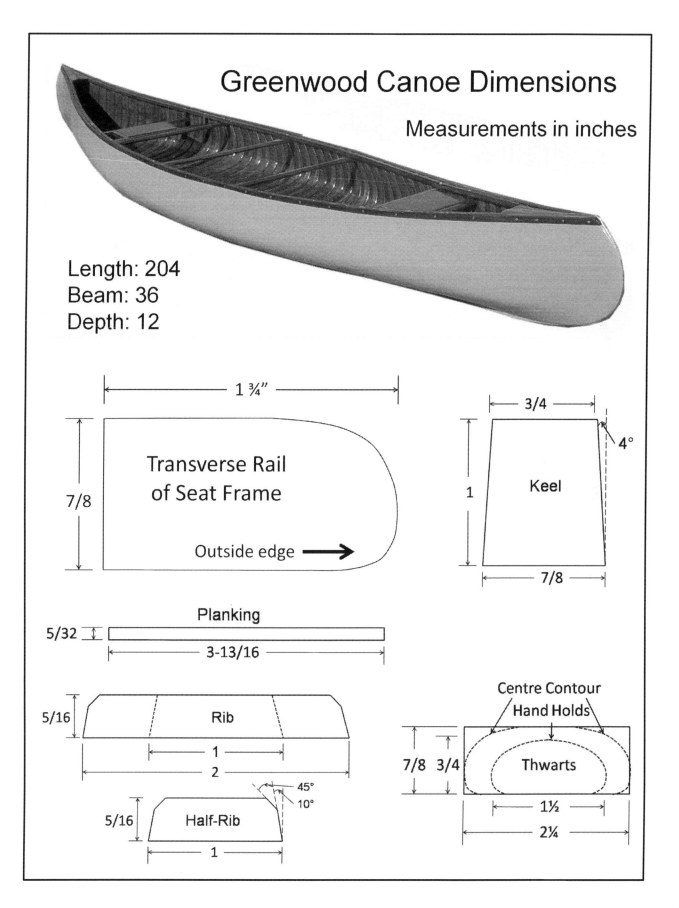

Greenwood Canoe Dimensions

Measurements in inches

Length: 204
Beam: 36
Depth: 12

Transverse Rail of Seat Frame

1 ¾"

7/8

Outside edge →

Keel

3/4

1

4°

7/8

Planking

5/32

3-13/16

Rib

5/16

1

2

Half-Rib

45°

10°

5/16

1

Centre Contour
Hand Holds

Thwarts

7/8 3/4

1½

2¼

Resources

The following resources include businesses I have dealt with and recommend. On-line resources include blogs and other sites providing information about wood-canvas canoes and related topics. The museums and associations are available for information through membership or subscription which is open to the public. The books listed are those referenced in this book but may not be in print. They may be available from libraries.

Associations and Museums

Canadian Canoe Museum
910 Monaghan Road
Peterborough, ON, K9J 5K4
705-748-9153
www.canoemuseum.ca

Wilderness Canoe Association
P.O. Box 91068
2901 Bayview Ave.
Toronto, ON, M2K 2Y6
www.wildernesscanoe.ca

Wisconsin Canoe Heritage Museum
P.O. Box 365
312 N. Front Street
Spooner, WI, 54801
715-635-5002
www.wisconsincanoeheritagemuseum.com

Wooden Canoe Heritage Association
P.O. Box 255
Paul Smiths, NY, 12970
603-323-8992
www.wcha.org

On-Line Sources

Canadian Canoe Routes
www.myccr.com/

Canoe Identification Guide
www.dragonflycanoe.com/id/index.html

CanoeGuy's Blog
http://canoeguybc.wordpress.com

Canoeroots Magazine
www.canoerootsmag.com

Kettle River Canoes
www.canoeshop.ca

7480 4th st.
Grand Forks
BC
V0H 1H0
Canada

Paddle Making
paddlemaking.blogspot.com

Playing with Boats
authenticboats.com

Song of the Paddle
www.songofthepaddle.co.uk

This Old Canoe
www.thisoldcanoe.com

Wooden Canoes and More
wwwbuckhorncanoes.blogspot.ca

Fasteners and Supplies

Allens Artist Canvas
3308 Preston Road Suite 350-192
Plano, TX, 75093
214-565-0029
www.allenscanvas.com
Untreated canoe canvas

Canadian Canoe Museum
910 Monaghan Road
Peterborough, ON, K9J 5K4
705-748-9153
www.canoemuseum.ca
Canadian canoe company decals

Canadian Tack and Nail 2003 Ltd.
431 Dundas St.
Cambridge, ON, N1R 5R5
519-622-0400
www.canadiantackandnail2003.com
Copper and brass canoe tacks and nails

Chichester, Inc.
2045 Niagara Falls Blvd., Unit 9
Niagara Falls, NY, 14304-1675
716-298-1183
http://www.chichesterinc.com
Rawhide canoe seat lacing

D. B. Gurney Company
746 Washington Street
Whitman, MA, 02382
781-447-4411
www.dbgurney.com
Brass canoe tacks

Faber & Co
2923 Rue de la Faune
Quebec, QC, G2A 3W8
418-842-8476
www.fabersnowshoes.com
Rawhide canoe seat lacing

Frank's Cane and Rush Supply
7252 Heil Avenue
Huntington Beach, CA, 92647
714-847-0707
www.franksupply.com
Natural rattan for hand-weaving seats

Jamestown Distributors
17 Peckham Drive
Bristol, RI, 02809
401-253-3840
www.jamestowndistributors.com
Marine supplies and fasteners

John Annesley Company
P.O. Box 181
Healdsburg, CA, 95448
707-433-4238
www.johnannesley.com
3" side-tack canvas pliers

Lee Valley Tools Ltd.
P.O. Box 6295, Station J
Ottawa, ON, K2A 1T4
613-596-0350
www.leevalley.com
woodworking tools and canoe tacks

Merton's Fiberglass & Marine Supply
314 Rocus Street
Springfield. MA, 01104
413-736-0348
10-24 silicon bronze carriage bolts

Northwoods Canoe Company
336 Range Road
Atkinson, ME, 04426
207-564-3667
www.wooden-canoes.com
canoe supplies and fasteners

Old Town Canoe Company
125 Gilman Falls Ave, Bldg B
Old Town, ME, 04468
207-827-5514
www.oldtowncanoe.com
canoe supplies and fasteners

Books

Bark Canoes and Skin Boats of North America
by Edwin Tappan Adney and Howard Irving Chappelle
(Re-published by Skyhorse
New York, NY 10018, 2007)

Building the Maine Guide Canoe
by Jerry Stelmok
(International Marine
Camden, ME, 1980)

Canoe Paddles
by Graham Warren and David Gidmark
(Firefly Books
Buffalo, NY, 2001)

Canoecraft
by Ted Moores and Merilyn Mohr
(Camden House
Buffalo, NY, 1983)

Fine Woodworking on Bending Wood
35 articles selected by the editors of Fine Woodworking magazine
(The Taunton Press
Newtown, CT, 1985)

Hand Tools: Their Ways and Workings
by Aldren Watson
(Portland House
New York, NY, 1982)

How to Restore Your Wooden Runabout
by Don Danenberg
(Motorbooks International
St. Paul, MN, 2003)

The Canoe: A Living Tradition
by John Jennings
(Firefly Books
Buffalo, NY, 2001)

The Furniture Doctor
by George Grotz
(Doubleday
New York, NY, 1962, 1983)

The Story of the Chestnut Canoe
by Kenneth Solway
(Nimbus Publishing Ltd
Halifax, NS, 1997)

The Wood & Canvas Canoe
by Jerry Stelmok and Rollin Thurlow
(Tillbury House
Gardiner, ME, 1987)

When the Chestnut was in Flower
by Roger MacGregor
(Plumsweep Press
Lansdowne, ON, 1999)

Zen and Japanese Culture
by Daisetz Suzuki
(Princeton University Press
Princeton, NJ, 1959)

Zen in the Art of Archery
by Eugen Herrigel
(Routledge & Kegan Paul Ltd
London, England, 1953)

Paddles

Badger Canoe Paddles
4362 Ravenscliffe Road
Huntsville, ON, P1H 2J2
705-783-6016
www.badgerpaddles.com

Grey Owl Paddles
62 Cowansview Road
Cambridge, ON, N1R 7N3
519-622-0001
www.greyowlpaddles.com

Shaw & Tenney, Inc.
P.O. Box 213 (20 Water Street)
Orono, ME, 04473
207-866-4867
www.shawandtenney.com

Notes

Notes

Notes